THE 4%

Dr Gerald Kushel

SIDGWICK & JACKSON
LONDON

First published in Great Britain in 1985
by Sidgwick & Jackson Ltd
Originally published in the United States
of America in 1984 by Contemporary Books Inc
under the title of *The Fully Effective Executive*

ISBN: 0 283 99174 7
Printed in Great Britain for
Sidgwick & Jackson Ltd, 1 Tavistock Chambers
Bloomsbury Way, London WC1A 2SG
by A. Wheaton & Co. Ltd., Exeter

Dedicated to:

- My wife, Selma
- My daughters, Joan and Lynne
- My father, Benjamin
- And to all those Executives,
  fully effective or not,
  whose sharing made this work possible

CONTENTS

ACKNOWLEDGMENTS

Thanks to my wife, Selma, for her consistent help, encouragement, and support in this project from beginning to end; to Dr. Roy L. Smith, for his help, especially in conceptualizing the Execupower Theory; to Richard Kaufmann, my associate at Execupower Associates, Inc.; and to Dr. Mel Heck, whose encouragement helped me to initiate this project. Thanks also to Maryann Bivona, for her extended clerical labors.

But most importantly, my appreciation to the hundreds of executives, fully effective or not, who took the time to share with me what goes on behind the executive mask.

G.K.
Melville, New York

1

INTRODUCTION:
Total Success

There are some persons who seem to have everything going for them—and sometimes they actually do. Total success, success in both work life and personal life is, as you might expect, an extremely rare commodity. But in a study that I have conducted over the past four years of 550 of America's top executives, I found a small group, only 4%, who were clearly enjoying an extremely high level of both personal and professional success. This was total, three-dimensional success. These highly effective executives not only had success in their jobs, with salaries ranging from 58 to 325 thousand dollars a year, but they also enjoyed their work very much. In addition, they had excellent personal lives which complemented their success at work.

It was this group, the Fully Effective Executives, that became the focus of my concentrated study over the last several years. How did they get so "Lucky"? What were their trade secrets, if any? And most importantly, were their methods for attaining and enjoying such a high level of total success transferable to other persons, persons perhaps such as yourself who are also seeking their own levels of three-dimensional success—a better job, more job satisfaction, and a pleasurable personal life?

My discoveries were most exciting. Not only did I learn how Fully Effective Executives (FEEs for short) got that way, but I learned all of their many trade secrets. Most exciting of all, I found that their approach, their methods for attaining such high levels of personal and professional success, were highly transferable to persons such as you and me—if we wanted to learn them! From my study of FEEs, I was able to formulate what I call the Execupower Theory. When put into practice, this theory becomes a system that anyone can use. The Execupower System is composed of one principle and six practices of FEEs. I will take you through this system, step by step, leading you carefully and easily to your own full measure of three-dimensional success, regardless of your present circumstances. All you need to do is put into action what I will explain to you in the following pages. In fact, once you understand how to employ the Execupower Principle and actually do so, the level of your own success will rise dramatically almost immediately.

In the next chapter, I'll tell you more about Fully Effective Executives and contrast them with their counterparts, the Self-Defeating and Semi-Effective Executives. After a brief introduction to some of the basics of the new Execupower Theory, I'll induct you immediately into the program—if you decide that you really want your own full measure of three-dimensional success.

2

THE *FULLY* EFFECTIVE EXECUTIVES (FEEs)

In my study of 550 top executives from all over the United States, I found that 16% were "self-defeating" (n = 88), 80% were "semi-effective" (n = 440), and only 4% were fully effective (n = 22).

Self-Defeating Executives, Semi-Effective Executives and, of course, Fully Effective Executives (FEEs) all held excellent jobs as indicated by their job titles, positions in their organizations, and high salaries. Yet the less effective executives were not enjoying the same *three*-dimensional success as the FEEs.

Self-Defeating Executives had impressive jobs but little job satisfaction, and their personal lives were in disarray. Semi-Effective Executives also had important, well-paying positions, and although they weren't quite as unsatisfied with their jobs or the quality of their personal lives, both of these dimensions were less than satisfactory. Of course, FEEs enjoyed all three dimensions of success: (1) an excellent, important, well-paying job, (2) enjoyment of that job, and (3) an excellent personal life as well.

In determining whether an executive was a Self-Defeating

3

Executive, a Semi-Effective Executive, or an FEE, several criteria were used. Each subject rated his or her personal life and work life in terms of the level of satisfaction.

Since each of the 550 subjects qualified by having an excellent, important job by virtue of their job title, rank, position in the organization, and high salary, no additional measures of job success were required. Selected subjects took the "Inner-Liberation Self Test," an instrument designed to measure levels of an individual's inner strength. FEEs scored in the top stanine in all of the criteria measured.

It was on 22 key executives who met all the criteria of Fully Effective Executives that became the focus of my concentrated study. Once judged an "FEE," each was subjected to an additional series of intensive interviews, formal and informal. In many instances, I also observed and studied their interaction in various small group activities. For example, as a trainer for the American Management Associations' Executive Effectiveness course, I met with various groups of executives for as long as 10 to 12 hours a day, for a week at a time. I have conducted this particular course in various parts of the United States, meeting with key executives from a wide range of corporations. Sessions were held at executive conference centers in such diverse areas as Williamsburg, Virginia; Tarpon Springs, Florida; Colorado Springs, Colorado; Hamilton, New York; Carmel, California; and Chicago, Illinois.

Below is a pseudonymous roster of the 22 Fully Effective Executives found in my study. The true identities, job titles, etc., have been completely disguised to protect the confidences that were shared during the course of my interviews and observations; but the levels of jobs, nature of business enterprises, etc., very closely approximate the real list. You will find many actual quotes from FEEs throughout the book.

Richard E. Barnes; Chief Executive Officer and Chairman of the Board of an outstanding national manufacturing concern.
Theodore G. Barton; Senior Partner of a well-known advertising agency.

Thomas C. Bennett; Senior Flight Systems Analyst of a rapidly expanding air freight company.

Kevin R. Blake; Senior Project Manager of a high-tech aerospace equipment company.

Laurence D. Burns; Chief Financial Officer of a major tool-and-die company.

Ronald C. Davies; President of a nationwide magazine publishing house.

Herbert S. Ditton; General Manager of a popular hotel-motel chain.

James T. Edwards; President of a very successful micro-electronics production company.

Neil F. Evans; Vice-President for an international conglomerate with heavy interests in the chemical industry.

James D. Geary; Executive Vice-President and Editor-in-Chief of a major metropolitan newspaper.

Edwin J. Hawser; Production Manager for a large U.S. steel producer.

Donald R. Heath; President of a very successful microcomputer company.

Vera L. Jennings; Chief of Administrative Services for a metropolitan medical center.

John C. Miller; Central Plant Manager and Chief Operating Engineer of a major textile manufacturing company.

Lawrence P. Owens; Chairman and Co-owner of a large chain of franchised seafood restaurants.

Loretta J. Reese; Vice-President in Charge of Sales for a major U.S. cosmetics firm.

Matthew P. Renolds; Chief Executive Officer of a large petroleum products concern.

Michael C. Richman; Director of Worldwide Strategic Planning for an international manufacturer.

T. Edward Rogers; TV Program Producer for a national TV network.

Phillip R. Roberts; Senior Actuary of a multi-billion dollar insurance company.

Robert J. Rosenberg; President of a high-fashion garment manufacturing concern.

Maxwell S. Vogel; Director of Legal Affairs of a large international finance corporation.

FEEs come in all shapes, sizes, and ages, and from all racial
and religious groups, and are of both sexes. They are scattered
widely throughout the American industrial complex—cities, sub-
urbs, and rural areas. They are found in all kinds of companies,
large and small, in manufacturing, banking and finance, electronics, aerospace, heavy equipment, publishing, in government, and
education—literally everywhere.

Their primary characteristic is that they are eminently successful, not only in their work, but also in how they feel about their
work and their lives in general. FEEs enjoy both their work and
their personal lives to the hilt. In addition to success in the
marketplace, they manage to have extremely pleasing private
lives, enduring and satisfying relationships with friends and family, and enjoy many quiet pleasures all alone.

Their tastes, however, vary considerably—in their desires for
family ties, friends, and recreational activities, etc. At work, they
are always among the most productive. They seek to win, and
usually do; although, as you shall see, they have a very special
definition of what winning means. FEEs always take full responsibility for their own actions and behavior and never, absolutely
never, foist the blame on others when something goes wrong.
They are highly realistic persons who always tackle reality head
on. As such, they are far removed from the stereotypically sugary
positive thinkers of the "Think Positive and Walk Over the Other
Guy" variety—the "Think Rich, Get Rich at Any Cost" types.
FEEs are down-to-earth pragmatic thinkers, and are never overly
self-righteous.

These unusually talented people have an uncanny knack for
practical problem solving, inevitably managing to skillfully reduce
anxiety-laden problems quickly into readily manageable projects.
They expertly divide all problems into their manageable parts so
that each part can be solved in turn. Hence, these most highly

successful of the successful have no real problems, only "manageable projects" underway.

Moreover, FEEs never take their work too seriously. They have an inner definition of themselves that goes far beyond their companies' job description, their job title, or even their families' definition of who they are. At work, they are more aptly described as gamesmen than as streetfighters. And they never allow themselves to become martyrs.

Although all of these FEEs operate in pressure cooker environments of competition and internal business politics, they have a unique way of looking at situations that turns ordinary distress, which often debilitates, into much more useful *eustress*. Eustress is a very positive creative tension that adds to their productivity, rather than detracting from it.

Although these persons have very powerful personalities, they seek to *influence* others rather then control them. They have great respect for their fellow workers, respecting most of all each individual's right and capacity to be fully responsible for his own deeds, feelings, and perceptions.

FEEs might sound like very imposing individuals, but if you were to meet an FEE, as you probably have, you might not know it. As neighbors, they often fit in easily. They are friendly, easy going, keep a relatively low profile, and are extremely helpful. But don't be misled by an FEE's exterior—they've always got ideas that are private, personal, and powerful. These ideas are the keys to their extraordinary success.

During the course of my interviews with them, I was often struck as to the difference between their inner lives and the appearance of their outer lives. As one FEE said, "It's a tough world out there. And if you go into it defenseless, you're bound to be hurt. What I've told you probably adds up to one big defense mechanism. But it's one that works for me and one that I love having." But even with their ready defenses, FEEs permitted themselves to be warm and vulnerable.

One other aspect of FEEs really struck me. Although each of them was zealous in pursuing a very satisfying life, they inevitably had as a personal policy that they would never attain their success *at the expense of any other person.* This was possible, as you'll soon see, because most attained their success through a winning *attitude,* not because they had to step on someone else to be a winner.

Here are some popular misconceptions about what it takes to be a total success. *None* of the following are characteristics of FEEs:

They're practitioners of positive thinking.

As hard-drivers, they really take their work, the company, and their career very seriously.

They foul up their personal and family life with their preoccupation with work and success.

They operate under great stress.

They have multiple problems weighing down on them every day.

They are real infighters.

They might look successful, but down deep they're really not.

They have a strong need to control others, their subordinates, peers, and, often, even those in positions above them.

When they know that they're right, they'll stick to their guns.

All of the preceding are sheer myths. The fact is that FEEs enjoy three-dimensional success without any of the above being true.

Many serious students of management are familiar with McGregor's Theory X and Theory Y (X = workers need to be prodded, Y = workers need to be treated compassionately), and most recently, the Japanese Theory Z (workers need to feel loyal and be able to zigzag their entire career with one company). Each of these theories has some utility, but now I'd like to introduce you to Theory E, the Execupower Theory. Theory E suggests that workers need to take total *self-responsibility.* Theory E also requires that everyone—boss, worker, peer, even family members—use their capacity to take total self-responsibility. With everyone exercising their maximum Execupower potential, both they, and the organizations they represent, will inevitably thrive.

The Execupower Theory was conceptualized inductively from my observations of FEEs' behavior and practices. Findings underscore two points: (1) All persons have enormous untapped power that can be released by taking total self-responsibility. (2) This power can be harnessed and used productively through the Execupower System. Hence, the Execupower Theory has been converted into a practical, easy-to-learn system, the Execupower System, the focus of this book. The system is based on only one principle and six practices, each derived entirely through my observation and study of FEEs. The Execupower System can be seen as a torch. The single principle forms the handle and base, and fuels the entire system. Each of the six common practices act as individual flames, which, when combined with the others, give off tremendous radiance, lighting the bearer's path to three-dimensional success.

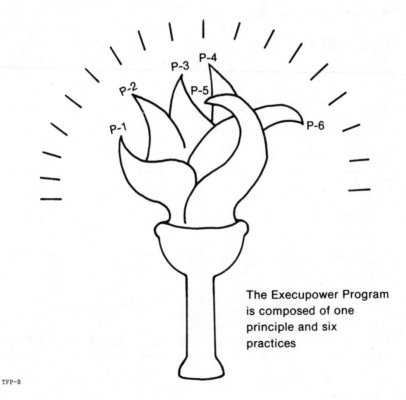

The Execupower Program is composed of one principle and six practices

It should be interesting for you to check your own current level of effectiveness by taking the following Fully Effective Self-Test. It is self-scoring, and after completion, you'll have an estimate of how you currently compare with the Fully Effective Executives. It will also serve as a diagnostic tool, indicating those specific areas that deserve your particular attention. Through Execupower, you will be able to give these special areas the attention that they require.

You can realistically expect that three weeks after you have completed the Execupower Program, your test scores will improve considerably, and the quality of your personal and professional life can be expected to improve accordingly.

The Fully Effective Self-Test

Instructions: Encircle the number on the line that most closely approximates how much you agree or disagree with each statement.

(1) I am currently enjoying a very high level of satisfaction in *both* my personal and professional life.

Agree   Disagree

9	8	7	6	5	4	3	2	1

(2) I know exactly what my primary personal goals are.

Agree   Disagree

9	8	7	6	5	4	3	2	1

(3) I know exactly what my primary professional goals are.

Agree   Disagree

9	8	7	6	5	4	3	2	1

(4) My work life and professional life do not interfere significantly with each other.

Agree								Disagree
9	8	7	6	5	4	3	2	1

(5) The primary source of my identity doesn't come from my job, my job title, or from my role in the family. I have a deeper sense of identity.

Agree								Disagree
9	8	7	6	5	4	3	2	1

(6) I tend to make most decisions easily.

Agree								Disagree
9	8	7	6	5	4	3	2	1

(7) I take self-responsibility, never blaming others for my thoughts, feelings, or behavior.

Agree								Disagree
9	8	7	6	5	4	3	2	1

(8) I am more of a realist than an idealist.

Agree								Disagree
9	8	7	6	5	4	3	2	1

(9) I currently have an important project underway, that is very much under my own control and not subject to significant outside interference. This project is very exciting and dear to me.

Agree								Disagree
9	8	7	6	5	4	3	2	1

(10) I can readily change those things that I have the power to change, whenever I choose to.

Agree   Disagree

| 9 | 8 | 7 | 6 | 5 | 4 | 3 | 2 | 1 |

(11) I can easily accept difficult situations and conditions over which I have little or no control.

Agree   Disagree

| 9 | 8 | 7 | 6 | 5 | 4 | 3 | 2 | 1 |

(12) I am certain that I know the difference between that which I can change and that which I cannot change.

Agree   Disagree

| 9 | 8 | 7 | 6 | 5 | 4 | 3 | 2 | 1 |

(13) I am currently involved in a program, formally or informally, to take good physical care of myself, including diet and exercise.

Agree   Disagree

| 9 | 8 | 7 | 6 | 5 | 4 | 3 | 2 | 1 |

(14) I never spite myself in order to get even.

Agree   Disagree

| 9 | 8 | 7 | 6 | 5 | 4 | 3 | 2 | 1 |

(15) I do not get unduly angry or worried.

Agree   Disagree

| 9 | 8 | 7 | 6 | 5 | 4 | 3 | 2 | 1 |

(16) I have a clear understanding of how the quality of my

listening influences others. I am particularly adept at listening to another person's feelings, when appropriate.

Agree								Disagree
9	8	7	6	5	4	3	2	1

(17) I think of myself as a loner even though I enjoy social activity.

Agree								Disagree
9	8	7	6	5	4	3	2	1

(18) I see myself as a risk taker.

Agree								Disagree
9	8	7	6	5	4	3	2	1

(19) Although I work hard at times, I am not a workaholic.

Agree								Disagree
9	8	7	6	5	4	3	2	1

(20) I am not overly concerned with others' approval of me.

Agree								Disagree
9	8	7	6	5	4	3	2	1

(21) I am determined to have one of the most satisfying personal and professional lives ever had by any human being that ever walked on the face of this planet, and I am succeeding in this ambition.

Agree								Disagree
9	8	7	6	5	4	3	2	1

(22) I know the difference between realistic and reasonable ex-

pectations and know how to balance these two in order to be most effective.

Agree   Disagree
9   8   7   6   5   4   3   2   1

(23) I deeply respect each and every person's right to take full responsibility for himself or herself.

Agree   Disagree
9   8   7   6   5   4   3   2   1

(24) I know what I have to do in order to manage my boss(es).

Agree   Disagree
9   8   7   6   5   4   3   2   1

(25) I have no unreasonable fears.

Agree   Disagree
9   8   7   6   5   4   3   2   1

(26) I generally tend to be a stress seeker rather than a stress avoider. Stress doesn't bother me as much as it seems to bother most persons.

Agree   Disagree
9   8   7   6   5   4   3   2   1

Scoring

Add up the numbers that you have circled. The following categories should give you an idea of how you compare with "Fully Effective Executives."

If your total is in the 208 to 234 range, you are currently enjoying a high level of personal and professional effectiveness. You should find this book quite reinforcing to your presently successful way of life. Those statements that you scored 7 or less reflect areas that need particular attention in order to improve your already high level of effectiveness.

If your total is in the 104 to 207 range, you are only partially effective—in the middleground. You can move either up or down. The Execupower System should prove extremely helpful to you in moving forward. Identify your weaknesses (items marked 7 or less) and concentrate on them as you move through the system, step by step.

If your total is in the 26 to 103 range, you are not using your innate Execupower capacity. Much of your effort seems self-defeating. This system can be expected to be of major significance to you and your personal and professional future. Follow each of the subsequent steps carefully and you will be able to break out of your less-than-effective cycle of functioning.

3

CHARTING YOUR SUCCESS GOALS

Here's a hypothetical conversation between an FEE and a friend:

"I've got one of the biggest jobs in the country. I don't know if you've heard about it. It's really a major responsibility."
"Really. Sounds terrific. What is it?"
"Well, I've just been appointed Chief Executive of a major organization."
"Terrific. Congratulations. What kind of organization?"
"It's a marvelous concern. It deals with people, human lives. Relationships. Also art and music. And entertainment. And building too. It also has something, actually quite a bit, to do with sex."
"Marvelous. Your job sounds absolutely fascinating. What a deal you've got. What is this job?"
"Hold on to your seat now. Don't fall over. Ready?"
"Sure. Go ahead, I'm ready."

"O.K. I've just been appointed Chief Executive in charge of Myself. And let me tell you, it's the most important job I've ever had in my entire life. The pay is excellent; it's the first job I've ever had where I get paid exactly what I deserve. If I excel, I get top dollar. If I goof off, I'm docked. Nothing could be fairer than that. I'm in charge of strategic planning, decision-making, accounting, operations, even sales. It's definitely a big responsibility, but I'm up to it. I'm even in charge of the physical fitness department and recreation. But my primary responsibility is to make the company a total success. I'm in top management—in charge of thoughts. They're the key to this entire operation. In this company, everything is controlled by thoughts. All feelings within this company can only come about after I, as C.E.O., decide on what thoughts to choose. And all activities of this company can take place in line with what I think. No one else can make a key decision. It's a tremendous responsibility all right. But what I like best is that I've got all the power I need to do a first rate job. It's a big job all right, being in full charge of a human being's life. But it's a very exciting assignment being Chief Executive in Charge of Myself!"

"Be careful what you set your sights on, for that's exactly what you are likely to get," said FEE Matt Renolds. FEEs make it their business to achieve their goals, so they give plenty of energy and attention to setting their professional and personal goals. Wake up an FEE at 3 a.m. and ask him to tell you immediately what his short, intermediate, and long-term professional goals are, and he'll be able to recite them to you, one, two, three. Ask him next, what his personal goals are and, even more rapidly, he'll tell you what they are. Moreover, the FEE will probably be able to give you the precisely ranked order of each of his goals. He always keeps his goals list up to date, constantly revising them in accordance with the changes that are taking place around him.

Whenever the FEE achieves a particular goal, he rests and enjoys deeply for a moment, but before long, he has conceptualized a new, exciting goal in place of the one that he's just realized. "Life is a journey, not an end," said FEE Max Vogel. "I enjoy the journey toward my goals even more than the actual achievement of them. Having exciting goals always makes my trip seem worthwhile."

The following exercises are designed to help you develop exciting, realistic goals for yourself. First, we'll examine some resentments that you might currently be harboring, resentments that may be preventing you from achieving all the success you're entitled to. You'll learn how to remove these roadblocks. Next, we'll take a complete inventory of your life history. It is your personal history that, up to now, has established the general direction in which you are moving. This direction might require some corrections and you'll be shown how to adjust your course, if necessary. Finally, we'll develop some very specific goals, exciting personal and professional goals that make eminent good sense for you. It's these goals, once you've committed yourself to them, that Execupower will help you attain.

Please complete the following sentences that begin with "About work, I resent . . ." If you are not currently on a payroll, but are a homemaker, a volunteer, or currently searching for "official" work, be sure to consider these activities as your work.

Please do not plan in advance what you are going to say before you answer. Your first impulse will have the most validity. Always write something to complete each of the following sentences, even if what you write is not clear to you at first.

About work, I resent ―――――――――――――――――――――――

About work, I resent ―――――――――――――――――――――――

About work, I resent ―――――――――――――――――――――――

About work, I resent ―――――――――――――――――――――――

Now complete the following sentences. These refer to resentments you might have about the quality of your personal life.

Again, please be spontaneous and be certain to complete each sentence.

About my personal life, I resent _____

_____

About my personal life, I resent _____

_____

About my personal life, I resent _____

_____

About my personal life, I resent _____

_____

Now review both lists. What noticeable themes or focal points seem to be emerging about you? Are your resentments primarily about other people? About yourself? About places, situations, and things? Can you think of any ways for reducing or eliminating these resentments? What steps are necessary to keep these resentments from spoiling your life?

Later on, when you compile your list of success goals, one of your goals should include bringing under control any resentments that are interfering with the quality of your life. Through Execu-power, you will see how each and every resentment that you have listed here can be completely eliminated. Although this may sound improbable, let me point out that FEEs never let resentments spoil their lives, and you can certainly learn how to do that too.

Next, take a full-size sheet of paper and draw a diagonal line from the lower left hand corner to the upper right hand corner. This line represents your personal/professional "lifeline."

Write your present age in the upper right hand corner where indicated. Then divide your lifeline into equal quarters. Write ¼ of your present age in the lower quarter. For example, if you are presently 36 years old, ¼ of 36 is 9. Therefore, write age 9, representing the first quarter of your life. Then ½ your present age (this would be ½ of 36, 18 in the example). And then ¾ of your present age, as indicated.

YOUR PERSONAL/PROFESSIONAL LIFELINE

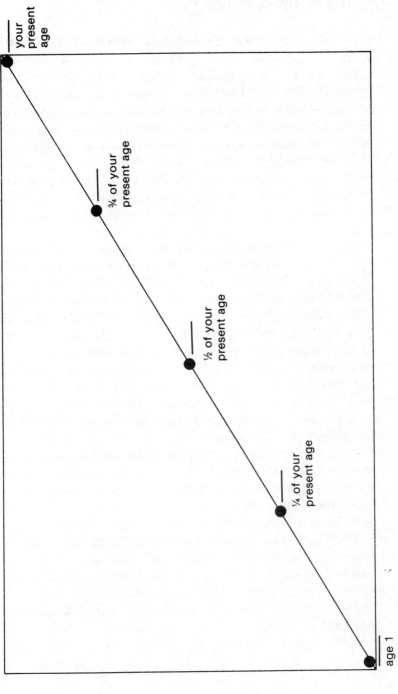

your present age

¾ of your present age

½ of your present age

¼ of your present age

age 1

Beginning with your earliest recollections, and using your own shorthand (phrases, letter, symbols etc.), make notes on your lifeline about as many specific incidents, events, and situations as you can recall. For example, if you were to remember that at age 12 your feelings were terribly hurt because you were not invited to an important party, or if you remember a marvelous vacation, then simply make a few shorthand notes on your lifeline. Later, we will review what you put on your lifeline.

Since no one other than you need ever see your shorthand notes, please be as forthright as you can possibly be. Continue up through the years of your life, marking your lifeline with appropriate notations of memorable events, situations, etc., as they occur to you. Write a notation of as many of these as come to mind right up until your present age, then stop. Rest for a few moments.

Now pause to contemplate this lifeline of yours. Take some time to consider such important questions as: Do you seem to have been primarily affected by people, situations, or material factors? Which seem to have been the most significant experiences in your life thus far? Identify, if you can, turning points in your life. Did your life change drastically at any particular point in time? If so, what caused this change? Are you headed in a positive or a negative direction at this point in time, as viewed from the perspective of your lifeline?

Most mature persons have gone through various stages or transitions in their lives. Identify two or three of these transitions for yourself and indicate them on your lifeline chart. It's often interesting to give each of these stages of your life an imaginative title, as if it were the chapter of a book. (Examples: "Years of Joy," "The Period of Both Agony and Ectasy," etc.) Write these titles above the various stages on your lifeline.

Now, once again contemplate your entire lifeline. Complete its various chapter titles. What do you make of your life thus far? Where have you been? Where are you now? Where are you heading?

At this point, pause and give your life an optimistic sounding title. Regardless of your past, predict a bright future for yourself.

Here are some possible book titles that project a successful future:

"Years of Pressure, Years of Glory"
"Becoming the Me that Never Was"
"Pathway to Success"
"Health, Unlimited"
"I Knew I'd Do It"
"Come Along, There's Room at the Top"
"Things Are Fine, but the Best Is Yet to Come"

It's important to choose a title that offers hope and includes an optimistic projection for your future. A title such as "Journey to Victory," "Venture to Inner Peace," or "I'll Definitely Make It," can become your own self-fulfilling prophecy. It would be self-defeating to prepare a scenario for yourself that doesn't include sufficient measures of personal and professional success.

We'll be referring to your book title periodically, so keep it in mind. Write it in the margin. Of course, always feel free to change your lifeline title as you see fit, but should you change it, always be sure that it includes plenty of optimism.

By attending to your past, you can derive insight into yourself and get some sense of the direction your life is taking.

Review your lifeline once again, and this time, identify by name one or two persons who seem to have made a special impression on you. Who were they? What were they like? Has anyone in particular ever served as a model or mentor for you, inspiring you to attain the very best that life has to offer? Is there an individual in your life who has a special knack for enjoying life? If so, what did you learn from this person? If you have not had such a person, don't be alarmed. FEEs can serve as valid and useful models if you sincerely want to improve the quality of each day remaining ahead.

FEEs offer an attitude of inestimable value that can help you transcend any inadequate models you might have had in the past.

Now let's go directly into goal setting. Complete the following sentences. Don't plan in advance what you say—act spontaneously. Please be sure to complete each sentence. Since this list is merely a worksheet, be as greedy as possible. It is not dangerous or evil to want. Of course, you might never get all that you want. But then again, with Execupower you might, so cut loose. We'll examine your responses after you've finished.

Now I desire _____

_____
Now I desire _____

_____
Now I desire _____

_____
Now I desire _____

_____

Complete the following sentences:

Within 6 months I want _____

_____
Within 6 months I want _____

_____
Within 6 months I want _____

_____
Within 6 months I want _____

_____

Finally, complete the following:

Eventually I want _____

_____
Eventually I want _____

_____
Eventually I want _____

_____
Eventually I want _____

_____

Look over your desires and wants—short, intermediate, and long-term. Are there significant differences between your long-term and your short-term desires? If so, what are these differences? To what extent are your desires primarily materialistic? Personal? Psychological? Do you feel satisfied or upset by what you see on your list? Why?

In order to reduce frustration, underscore only those desires that are achievable. It's all right for a particular want to be a long shot, but it should still be within the realm of possibility. It doesn't hurt to have fantastic dreams, but it isn't usually wise or necessary to stake everything you've got on achieving them. Keep wild dreams in reserve, but be sure to accomplish all of your achievable dreams and goals, then set new ones.

With Execupower you'll be certain to have an extremely satisfying personal and professional life. All FEEs have established, as their first major objective, having an extremely satisfying life. This objective, "a terrific life," is never removed from the FEE's consciousness. However, many less effective persons often don't believe that such a goal is realistic or attainable, except by accident. Yet FEEs make it happen.

Do you really believe that it is realistic or possible for you to have an outstanding personal-professional existence? Many persons that I've counseled erroneously believe that no one is truly happy or totally enjoying their lives. "Life is very hard," they say. "No one can have it all. Whenever I get to know one of those so-called 'happy-types' close up, I inevitably find that down-deep, they're not really enjoying themselves nearly as much as they pretend. If they are doing okay at work, then their family life is screwed up. If their family life is okay, then there's still something else that's wrong. Behind almost every successful man is an unhappy wife or screwed up kids." But this perspective is not supported by the evidence that I gathered in my study of FEEs.

FEEs never rule out the possibility of "three-dimensional success." Less effective persons wrongly hypothesize they'll never be that lucky. Since they so readily believe it, they immediately become victims of their own self-fulfilling prophecy. Attaining the high level of personal-professional satisfaction that is enjoyed by FEEs is not a matter of luck—it is a matter of application. No one is born to be unsuccessful. Lack of success may very well

TFP–C

have been programmed into persons by well-meaning parents, friends, or educators who didn't know any better. But Execu-power can change all that. Execupower will program out "lack of success" as a lifestyle and program in "total success."

Therefore, if you haven't done so already, be sure to establish for yourself as your top priority goal the objective of having "one of the most satisfying personal and professional lives ever had by any human being that ever walked on the face of this earth." If you keep this as your primary objective, using Execupower will virtually guarantee that you'll attain it.

All other goals that you set for yourself should be subordinate to this primary objective. Say to yourself: "I hereby solemnly swear that I will have as my number one, top priority goal, for each and every day remaining in my life, the attainment of *the most satisfying personal/professional life ever had by any human being that ever lived.*" As one FEE explained, "ever since I set my sights on having tremendous personal and professional success, I've had an infinitely better life than the one I was having before. I may not be the *most* satisfied person to have ever lived, but I'm certainly doing a hell of a lot better than I used to. And believe me, it's been lots more pleasurable working toward this goal than some of the others much less achievable that I've worked toward. This one makes great sense to me. It's worth attaining." Since less effective persons often do not believe that such a wonderful goal is even possible, they fail to vigorously pursue it. But satisfaction must be pursued with vigor, if it is to be attained. My research of FEEs shows that total success is not only possible but can be readily achieved by those who know how to go about it.

Now, taking into account all of your desires, resentments, past history, and all the thinking about these that you have just done, complete a five-year projection for yourself. Be sure to make some optimistic predictions since you will have a tendency to make your prophecies come true. Be realistic and confident. Execupower will help you make any plan become a reality. And if you want to change your plans later, you can do that too, any time you desire.

Tentative Five-Year Plan

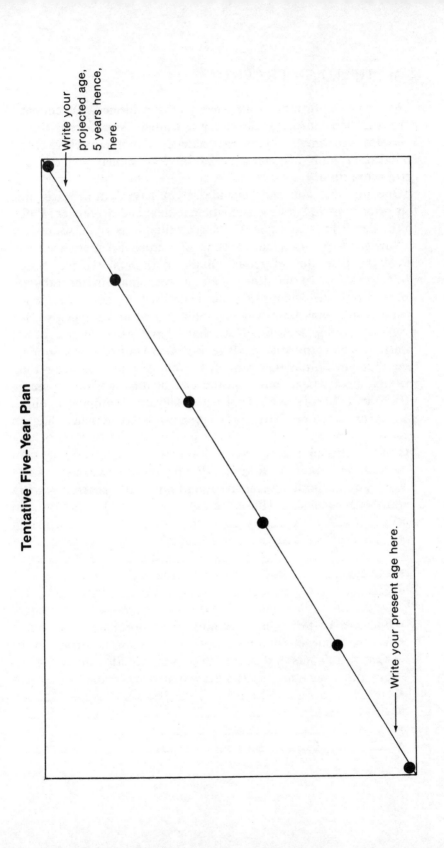

Write your projected age, 5 years hence, here.

Write your present age here.

Are you comfortable with what you've projected? Of course, even the best of plans can be interrupted by poor health, a wayward economy, and overdependency on others. Have you included in your projects some exciting goals that you can be certain to attain?

One goal that you must include, if you haven't done so, is the top priority goal, "having a terrific personal and professional life to the day I die." That goal is 100% attainable as you'll soon see.

Now please put your success goals in writing. Take into account all of the preceding exercises completed thus far. In the space provided below, write down your success goals in the ranked order of priorities. Complete a separate list for short-term, intermediate, and long-term success goals. Some of your goals will probably overlap each list. Note that I have taken the liberty of inserting the top priority goals of FEEs on your lists. It's important that you initial this goal if you can accept it as your top priority success goal, too. I promise that although it may seem very lofty, a "terrific life" is entirely achievable and realistic, once you learn how to properly apply Execupower to your own life.

My short-term goals are:
- To have one of the most satisfying days and weeks ever had by any person that ever lived, and not at the expense of any other person. _____ (Please initial if you agree.)
- _____
- _____
- _____
- _____
- _____

My intermediate-term goals (six months or more) are:
- To have one of the most satisfying six-month periods ever had by any person that ever lived, and not at the expense of any other person. _____ (Please initial if you agree.)
- _____
- _____
- _____
- _____

My long-term goals are:
- To have one of the most satisfying lives ever had by any person that ever lived, and not at the expense of any other person. _____ (Please initial if you agree.)
- _____
- _____
- _____
- _____

And now, presuming that your success goals are fixed as clearly as possible in your mind, let's move directly to the master key of the Execupower System—the *one* principle that all FEEs have in common—the Execupower Principle.

4

THE EXECUPOWER
PRINCIPLE

Harry Truman first said it, although he only meant it politically, not personally. FEEs use the principle politically, personally, and professionally. They use it whenever they need it. It is, in fact, the very key to their extraordinary level of three-dimensional success: "The buck stops here," said President Truman, and that, in essence, is the principle. Other Americans, Emerson and Thoreau, also took self-responsibility quite seriously. Thoreau put the self-reliance principle into practice at Walden Pond. It's an old, though often forgotten American ideal.

Without exception, all FEEs take total, complete self-responsibility for their thoughts, feelings, and actions. They never blame anyone or anything else. That's the very essence of Execupower.

FEE Jim Edwards, a company president, articulated the self-responsibility doctrine:

"Certainly I take much of the credit for the success that this company has had since I've been its president. But I also take the blame for the things that went wrong. Blaming here always stops at my desk. That's the way it is. Obviously it's easy to accept the kudos for success, but a person should also be able to handle the flak too, when it comes. And it comes quite often when you're in the catbird seat." Edwards not only took full responsibility for his business activities, but applied the self-responsibility doctrine to his personal life as well.

"One evening," Edwards said, "I came home tired from work only to find my Esther emotionally distraught. I didn't know what was wrong and, when I asked her, she just wept and repeated what I had heard many times before, that the kids were acting obnoxious and were driving her crazy, the house was on her nerves, and literally everything about our marriage was making her feel desperately trapped. Right off, I could feel myself getting a surge of anger. Just as I was about to yell 'Damn it, Esther, I've heard all this before. Please stop it,' and proceed to lecture 'her on why she had no business feeling the way she said she did, I suddenly caught myself and stopped. Instead of becoming defensive and launching my usual attack, I stopped, and then I reminded mysel', 'Jim, you'd better really listen to Esther. I mean really listen to her this time. I think she means business.'

"So Esther and I went into the den for some privacy, where the kids couldn't hear us, and for the first time in years, I really listened to her. I listened intensely and with plenty of feeling as she cried and as she told me step-by-step about all the pressures she was feeling—pressures of managing the house, the kids, shopping, handling repairmen, everything.

"I even paid attention, without defending, as she shared her resentments about my mother. She's never liked my mother. I gave to Esther the warmest attention possible. I listened, not so much to the content of what she was saying, although that was important too. I listened mostly to her feelings. I tried to appreciate her as a person. I tried to place myself in her shoes. And I think I came pretty close to feeling with her.

"It wasn't just this one time that I paid attention to Esther this special way. I made caring a matter of habit. And after awhile my caring began to have a very positive effect on our relationship.

You see, having a close relationship with my wife is extremely important to me.

"Together, Esther and I figured out some positive steps that we could take to lift some of the pressures that she was feeling. My listening, without defending, apparently showed her that I really cared, that I really could appreciate and care for her on her terms. Esther and I have become a whole lot closer these days. Sure, we were drifting apart, but what I did brought us much closer together. And as you know, if a guy has warm, close relationships at home, it helps him in his business too. Now I go to work in the morning with a clear head."

When Jim Edwards *stopped,* then proceeded to assume responsibility for curbing his "instinctive" impulse to defend himself, and chose to listen deeply to his wife, he was intuitively employing what I call the Execupower Principle.

The Execupower Principle requires the surrender of one of the most highly cherished defense mechanisms known to man—the convenience of blaming others when things go wrong. Most executives and other persons too (about 96%, according to my studies) are unwilling to let go of this self-defeating defense.

Yet, the cost for retaining it, convenient as it might be on occasion, is much too high. Keeping it requires that you give up all hopes of ever attaining all of the personal and professional power that FEEs enjoy. FEEs never blame as an excuse. Instead, they tell themselves that "Neither he, she, it nor they ever make me feel this way. Rather, it's the thoughts I choose that do the trick, that make me feel terrific or make me feel sick."

FEEs have a wide range of strategies available to handle any given situation, no matter how difficult. Therefore, it appears senseless for them to shirk self-responsibility. FEEs for example, never permit themselves to become mere victims, no matter what the situation. FEE Loretta Reese: "I always refuse to think of myself as a martyr even if I've been wronged. Martyrdom might be all right for somebody else, but not for me. Although it might sometimes appear to others as though I'm a victim, believe me, I never feel that way personally. There's no payoff in that for me."

FEE Don Heath: "When the Japanese saturated our computer markets and the demand for our instruments decreased, I took charge. Let's face it, it was stupid for us to have expanded our microcomputer line with competition being what it was just then. Very poor timing on our part—a result of a stupid decision, and as it happened, it was largely *my* decision. Look, it's my job to make smart decisions. That's what I'm paid for, smart decisions, not dumb ones. So I made a stupid mistake, and I quickly admitted it. Fortunately, we've been able to bounce back from that fiasco. I realize that everyone doesn't always get a second chance, but I managed to get one, and I used that second chance to come out even stronger in the long run. I've always learned from my mistakes. I might make them every so often, but I almost never repeat them. When you can't take the heat for your mistakes, then it's time to get out. Who knows, maybe someday I'll get fired. But you know what? If it ever came to that, that wouldn't throw me either. I feel as if I can handle anything. Even disasters. Look, everything worked out okay for me and the company and I've since become president of the whole damned operation. For me, there's no question that I owe most of my so-called success to my taking of self-responsibility."

Another FEE, Bob Rosenberg, used the taking of self-responsibility to control his formerly outrageous temper: "I had a tendency to get very uptight. Business wasn't very good and I was taking it out at home. I heard Timmy, my youngest, warn his brother, 'Watch out for Dad, he's on the warpath.' At that point, I simply stopped, took an inventory of what I was doing, and figured out that it was due to my faulty attitude. So I changed my attitude and did what I had to to keep from needlessly upsetting my family. The way I figured it, I alone was making myself angry. It wasn't really business conditions that was doing it to me. I was doing it to me." This "I can take care of it" attitude was pervasive throughout all my interviews with FEEs, from the most seasoned to the youngest rookie.

THE EXECUPOWER PRINCIPLE STATED FUNCTIONALLY

The Execupower Principle—stated in functional terms, a way

that you can quickly use it for yourself—is: "**Whenever necessary /pause/then choose/fully effective thoughts.**" Each segment of this principle has a special meaning, the significance of which we shall review in detail shortly. At first, however, it's very important that we examine the principle as a whole, so as to sensitize you to its enormous potential as a vehicle to success.

FEE Jack Miller felt extremely nervous just as he was about to enter the boardroom to make a major address at the annual stockholders meeting. "Now is definitely not the time to feel nervous," he thought to himself. So Miller quickly took charge, paused, then chose certain very effective thoughts so that he could deliver his talk in top form. Miller concentrated on those ideas that he knew would make him feel calm. He reminded himself that he was well-informed on the subject matter of his talk, that he had the capacity to think spontaneously on his feet, that he had been through all of this before, many times, and had always risen to the occasion.

In this manner, Miller proceeded to think his way into an excellent, calm, confident disposition. Then at the appointed moment, Miller strode confidently into the boardroom— reinforced and supported by his own confident thinking—and delivered one of his best talks ever.

For some persons, rather than calm down, it behooves them to get excited before a talk. What is effective thinking for one person may not be at all for another. Effective thinking is quite idiosyncratic.

Without question, you will feel absolutely nothing in your body without a correlative thought. A football hero runs 80 yards for a winning touchdown before a cheering crowd of thousands. "I feel fantastic," he says. "But look Charlie," his teammate points out, "your arm is broken and your nose is a bloody mess." "My god, I didn't feel a thing," the hero says in dismay, "I never gave it a thought." Obviously since his mind was totally on scoring the touchdown, he didn't notice any pain. It is not the injuries that cause the pain, but a person's thoughts acknowledging the pain that cause it. It's the same principle that permits yogis to lie comfortably on a bed of nails.

Elaine didn't learn of her best friend's death until the morning after her friend had died. Naturally it wasn't until after Elaine learned of her friend's passing that she felt upset and remorseful. Again, it was not the event that caused the feelings. It was Elaine's thoughts about the event that upset her. Clearly then, feelings cannot exist without a correlative thought. Early Greek philosophers noted this fact in their literature, and Shakespeare also wrote. "There is nothing good nor bad, that thinking doesn't make it so."

Jack was automatically infuriated at being poked and jolted by the obviously rude person behind him who pushed to get out of the elevator. "Bastard, take you're time," Jack thought angrily to himself. But when he turned around and saw that the man poking him was blind, his thoughts on the matter changed completely. In an instant, Jack recognized that the blind man was only doing the best he could, considering his serious handicap. As his thoughts changed, so did his feelings. His fury immediately ceased and in its place Jack felt pangs of genuine compassion for this blind man's plight. Consequently, Jack offered the blind man assistance so that he could exit safely from the elevator. At the risk of belaboring the point, I note once again that thoughts precede feelings. This is an extremely important point to remember.

Feelings never exist in a vacuum. This point is so central to the Execupower Principle that it is worth reminding yourself of it time and again. Very often we forget and convince ourselves that our feelings just drop in on us from out of the sky, as if we were nothing but the victims of a condition which we can do very little about. Yet, as every FEE knows, that's simply not true.

The Choice Is Always Yours: Use Execupower

Situation: You're feeling the pressure from work. You want to blame the job.

Self-Defeating Thought	**Fully Effective Thought**
My work is really making me upset.	I'm choosing upsetting thoughts about my work. I'm making myself upset.

Thoughts not only create feelings, but behavior as well. You can have no meaningful behavior without a correlative thought, a thought that produces the behavior. In order for me to type this sentence right now, thought is required to move my fingers properly on the keyboard. Although the thought may be deeply ingrained and habitual when it comes to typing words, very active thought processes are necessary for these words to appear in a meaningful sentence.

As human beings, we are a combination of various thoughts, feelings, and behaviors. Thoughts are the most significant since without them feelings and meaningful behavior could not possibly exist. Feelings, of course, are very important too, for it is in the realm of feelings (that which goes on under our skin) that we actually live. Feelings are undeniably real. Behavior is very important also. But psychologically, behavior is only the tip of the iceberg. Behavior is the small part of a person that goes public. Since no one can actually see our thoughts or our feelings, our behavior often gets most of the attention of others. But as valuable as actions and behavior are, FEEs concentrate most of their energies on the thoughts that they choose.

Thought is at their executive center. It is our thoughts that cause us to feel all emotions, including depression, anxiety, joy, vitality, and fatigue. If FEEs want to change their feelings, they simply change the thoughts that they choose.

The Execupower Principle, **"Whenever necessary/pause/then choose/fully effective thoughts,"** is in four distinct segments: (1) Whenever necessary (2) Pause (3) Then Choose and (4) Fully Effective Thoughts. It's necessary to thoroughly examine each segment separately so you can completely master this valuable sentence.

Segment 1. "Whenever Necessary"

"Whenever necessary" refers to the fact that FEEs are doggedly determined to have one of the most satisfying lives ever had by any human being that ever walked on the face of the earth, never at the expense of any other person. Since this goal is always in the back of their minds, they are particularly sensitive to those times when the feelings they are experiencing are not in keeping with this fundamental commitment they have made to themselves.

For example, when suffering at an interminably boring meeting, they suddenly notice what they are doing to themselves. They notice that they are struggling to pay attention to a colleague's tedious presentation that is entirely predictable—a presentation that they've heard time and time again. At this point the FEE stops to pause. He says to himself, "Wait a minute, this meeting isn't boring me. It's the fact that I'm trying so hard to listen to this tedious ego trip that so and so is going through that's boring me half to death. But I don't have to sit here and suffer. I can sit here and enjoy, just by thinking of something pleasurable. I wasn't put on this planet to suffer." FEE Jim Edwards: "I never forget, even for a moment, that I have but one life, that I'm only passing this way once, and I intend to make this trip through as successful a trip as is humanly possible."

The Choice Is Always Yours: Use Execupower

Situation: You're finding that you're not living up to your commitment to have a very satisfying inner life.

Self-Defeating Thought	Fully Effective Thought
There's nothing I can do about it. I'm a victim of a difficult situation.	There's plenty I can do about this. I'm never a victim. This is "whenever necessary time" to choose thoughts that create inner satisfaction in spite of what's going on "out there." I've got a deep commitment to myself to always live a very satisfying inner life.

Suppose that you knew before you were born that your entire life was going to last only five minutes. What kind of life would you choose? Probably one that would give you satisfaction. Certainly not one filled with torment and tension. Nor would you choose a life filled with depression, or one plagued with feelings of guilt, unless you were a masochist. If you chose the life of complete inner satisfaction, all that you would have to do would be to choose thoughts that gave you inner satisfaction for only five minutes.

You could use up one or two minutes visualizing the beauty of the setting sun, or just thinking about having fantastic sex with your favorite sex symbol. Another minute or two could be spent thinking about the pleasures of winning the sweepstakes, imagining that you've just been made Chairman of the Board of IBM, or pretending that you've just hit a home run with the bases loaded and you're rounding third base and waving to the 75,000 cheering fans. The last few moments could be devoted to enjoying your favorite music, viewing a superb work of art, or whatever else you choose to think about to give you inner pleasure.

Of course, real life is hopefully much longer than five minutes, but you can decide to live it in units of five satisfying minutes at a time if you want to. Life is hard, but yard by yard, inch by inch, it's a cinch. It's "whenever necessary time" anytime you become aware that you are not living up to your potential.

Imagine that you and a traveling companion had just driven 1,000 miles in order to view the grandeur of the Grand Canyon at sunset. You arrive just ten minutes before sunset. Moments before stepping out of your car, however, you become embroiled in a heated, thoroughly nonproductive, yet highly emotional argument with your traveling companion. Obviously, this is a "whenever necessary" time. It's time to put Execupower into action. In keeping with your vow to get the most out of life, it makes no sense to spoil the beauty you've traveled so far to see by continuing to argue.

The sun is rapidly setting; time is clearly of the essence. Some foolish persons would continue the argument, or at least continue to be upset and let the argument spoil the pleasure of the view. But no FEE that I know would ever do that. Instead, at such a moment, FEEs stop arguing and pause.

Segment 2. "Pause"

The pausing is a crucial part of the Execupower Principle. Let's return to that hypothetical argument you were having with your traveling companion just as you were about to embark from your car to view the Grand Canyon at sunset. Since the sun is rapidly setting, you've only got a short time to get your act together.

The Choice Is Always Yours: Use Execupower

Situation: The sun is setting. You're going to miss this spectacular sight if you don't bring your emotions immediately under control.

Self-Defeating Thought
I can't calm down. It takes time. I'll never be able to do it.

Fully Effective Thought
I'll put a stop to my emotional upset immediately. I'll pause, calm down, and focus on the beauty of the view. I'll get to that unfinished emotional business later, after the sunset.

Here are some important considerations that can take place during "pause." You can balance your psychological compass. You can remind yourself that continuing to feel upset during the ensuing moments will most certainly defeat your primary objective "to enjoy life to the hilt." You can quickly review your various options: Option 1: You can continue feeling upset, and continue the argument. (You'll undoubtedly discard this option immediately as it has little value.) Option 2: You can try to resolve the argument before the sunset. (This may be close to impossible.) Option 3: You can table your argument until after you've viewed and enjoyed the scene. (You can then concentrate on the beautiful natural phenomenon in front of you.) Finishing the argument can wait. Obviously this is the wisest option in view of the circumstances, and the one that undoubtedly would be chosen by FEEs. Although options 1 and 2 might have had merit in other contexts, they are not very attractive here.

"Pausing" is what the high-diver does as he steps to the end of the board and stops momentarily before deftly executing a beautiful double jackknife. "Pausing" is what the pitcher does just before he winds up for that crucial bases-loaded pitch with Reggie Jackson staring him in the face. At the "pause," the athlete stops momentarily, composes himself, then cuts loose into optimal action.

One excellent use of "pausing" is to break the pattern of a self-defeating mindset. It's your basic mindset that determines what you see in a given situation. Try the following mindset exercises, then check the correct answers at the end.

1. What is this?

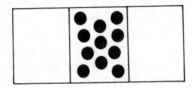

2. Please connect all nine dots, drawing only four straight lines, without doubling back or lifting your pen from the paper.

3. Which is longer, the *brim* or the *peak* of this hat?

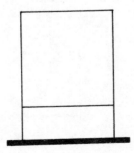

4. Which is correct, 9 + 7 *is* 17? Or 9 + 7 *are* 17?

Answers:
1. A giraffe walking past a window.
2. Go beyond the imaginary boundary that the symmetry of the dots seems to have established:

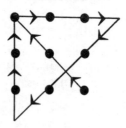

3. Both are *exactly* the same length.
4. Neither: 9 + 7 = 16.

We can be duped by a self-defeating mindset. However, in accord with Execupower Theory, you have the capacity to choose any mindset you want, anytime or place that you want to.

For example, in the Necker Cube below, you can choose to see the cube projecting *up* or *down* depending on how you want to view it.

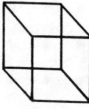

Mindset projecting the cube upward

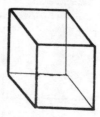

Mindset projecting the cube downward

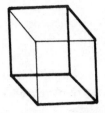

Much of the quality of your life depends entirely on your point of view. Look at the number 35 as it is perceived from ground level, and then as it is seen from the air. The number 35 hasn't really changed, but the different point-of-view certainly changes the way it appears.

Perception from the ground   Perception from the air

FEE Matt Renolds: "Attitude isn't everything. It's the *only* thing."

Sometimes mindsets can really make us look foolish. Recently I was driving on a long trip upstate and my mind was very busy. Suddenly I found myself at the highway toll booth. In my left window, there appeared the face of a man in some kind of uniform. "Fill er up," I said without *pausing*. If I had paused, balanced my compass, and changed my mindset to reality, I'd have avoided that silly comment. When you "pause," consider your options, then *choose* the option that has the greatest payoff for you. It's always your choice.

Segment 3. "Then Choose"

All FEEs believe in free will. They are absolutely convinced that they have the power to *choose* any thought that they want, at any time and any place.

FEE Jack Miller: "Someone can always *order* me to act a certain way, or even require that I be in a particular place, especially at the plant. Others can even require that I spew the party line, building up the company and so forth. But absolutely no one on this earth, other than myself, can guarantee that I will *choose* a particular thought. I reserve the right to pick any thought I want to, at any time and at any place. Choosing what I want to think is my one inalienable right as a human being. No one can ever take that right away from me. Not the Chairman of the Board, not the President of the United States, not even my wife or kids. *Choosing* thoughts belongs entirely to me. It may, in fact, be the only absolute freedom that I really have. And no one, except me, can take that freedom from me."

Dr. Viktor Frankl, a renown psychiatrist, was imprisoned in Nazi concentration camps. He later wrote, "The ultimate freedom of man is the freedom to *choose* one's own attitude, regardless of external circumstances." It was through a conscious and systematic program of "thought-choice" that Frankl enabled himself to survive the bestial and inhuman treatment given him by the Nazis. If Frankl could choose any thought he wanted in a concentration camp, we can certainly do it where we are.

Some philosophers argue that there is really no such thing as free will. They contend that man's capacity to choose is only an illusion, created by those who have insatiable egos. They believe that human beings are mere victims of fate, of cause/effect determinism.

However, the exciting and successful lives of FEEs, who base their success primarily on their will to choose, serve to overrule that sterile notion. FEE Michael Richman, in discussing his capacity to choose his own thoughts, said, "Yes, I might very well be kidding myself that I'm in charge of my life. That is a possibility. It may very well be true that I am nothing more than a hopeless victim in an endless chain of causes and effects, that I only have an illusion that I'm in charge. But since I'm the world's best expert on the quality of my own life, let me tell you that it is a pleasure living with the delusion that I'm a very special being, that I'm a free agent, totally in charge of the quality of my personal existence. Since I prefer to believe that I have choices and since that works best for me, why should anyone want to prove to me that I'm nothing more than a victim of cause and effect?"

Most depressed persons either do not know how to or do not want to assume the responsibility that attends the choosing of their own thoughts. Instead, they go out of their way to find sufficient reason to believe that they are hopelessly trapped, with no apparent way out other than a change in external circumstances or conditions. Although FEEs believe, as others do, that they are often compelled to be in situations not of their own choosing, they differ in that they stubbornly resist feeling trapped. Consequently they cleverly design means and programs to find their way out of life's boxes. Although this is not always possible physically, it is always possible attitudinally.

It is true that thoughts often seem to burst forth, appearing to rise up magically from one's subconscious. But since your subconscious has been programmed much like a computer by parents, relatives, friends, even an enemy or two, it is prudent to be on guard. If the thoughts that happen to rise up "automatically" are in concert with your fully effective purposes, fine; but on those special occasions when self-defeating, defective, counterproductive thoughts rise up, thoughts that are ulcerating or insufferable, it's time to exercise your Execupower option and *willfully* choose thoughts that have a greater payoff.

You should always have at your ready disposal a number of thought-choice options. You can always *choose* what you will hear and what you will not hear. You can always *choose* to love anybody that you want to love, regardless of whether or not they choose to love you in return. You can *choose* to think about religion in any way that you so desire. You can *choose* to think about having passionate sex with anyone your heart desires—a movie star, a new acquaintance, or a long-time lover. Of course, you can't always act on what you choose to think.

Though you may not be able to act any way that you want, any time and place that you choose, you can definitely think and consequently feel any way that you want, at any time or place. This gives you tremendous personal power since your thoughts create your feelings.

For example, if your boss insists that you think primarily about business matters during your free time, it's up to you to decide whether or not you'll actually go along with his demand. No one need ever know what you really think. Not your boss, your mother, or anyone else, if that's what you decide. No one other than you rules what you choose to think. Your boss might order you to think about work in your spare time. You always reserve the right to decide whether you wish to comply with such a request. Instead, you might choose thoughts about the pleasures of sunbathing, strolling on the beach, enjoying the theater, or even reliving the pleasures of a recent sexual experience, if such thoughts interest you. No one need ever know but you. How unfortunate it is that many persons do not enjoy this readily available power, the power to choose thoughts that are productive or fun.

Puppies, dogs, lions, elephants, and all other animals have no choices; they are limited to their basic instincts and are the products of conditioning. Even though the Russian experimenter, Pavlov, easily trained his dog to salivate upon hearing a bell, we need not become victims of such conditioning. A human can interpret the sound of the bell with a thought-choice; he can interpret the bell to mean anything he wants.

Advertising commercials, slogans, and mass media campaigns aim at having us think and buy like conditioned animals. But FEEs resist such conditioning. FEE Loretta Reese: "The song lyric, 'You made me love you' is sheer nonsense. No one can actually *make* another love them. We always have a choice. Lt. Calley, in Vietnam, could not really hold those above him in the chain of command responsible for what he did. Even if he was ordered to pull the trigger on innocent Vietnamese, it was he alone who pulled the trigger on his gun." FEEs contend that all those worthy of the title "human being" are completely responsible for all of their own thoughts, feelings, and behavior.

Rene Descartes, the philosopher, wrote: "I think, therefore, I am." He contended that without thought a person does not really exist, that without thought we are little more than vegetables.

The driver who hogs the highway in front of you can make you angry only if you choose anger producing thoughts from the many thought-options available to you. When a less than fully effective executive sees that his secretary has carelessly over-booked his appointment schedule, it seems only natural that he become angry and upset. "After all," the self-defeating executive reasons, "any normal, red-blooded executive would be angry too in such circumstances." But where is it written that one must get angry in any given circumstance?

FEEs, in a similar circumstance, often choose calming thoughts rather than anger-producing ones. They curb their automatic inclination, if necessary, and follow a line of thinking such as: "Since my secretary has overbooked me, I'll deal effectively with the given right now, and later on I'll show her a system that will prevent her overbooking my schedule next time. What steps do I need to take to take care of today's screw-up? What appointments have the highest priority? Which have to be rescheduled? What's the very worst that can possibly happen? How will I deal with the worst that can happen?" Clearly, such a productive line of think-ing is infinitely more self-serving than excessive anger that only upsets. If acting angry were to be of value, it would not be beyond the FEE's ability to pretend that he was upset. But when excessive anger in the work place is unnecessary, the FEE chooses nonanger-producing thoughts.

Follow this logic: S = Stimulus, R = Response, and $\widehat{TC}$ = Thought–Choice. S→R (Stimulus→Response) is the traditional way of diagramming stimulus/response. A given stimulus, ac-cording to behavioral psychologists produces a predictable re-sponse in pigeons, rats, and guinea pigs; this applies only to the lower animals, those that have no thought-choices. Since FEEs and other human beings can willfully choose their own thoughts, the traditional S→R diagram must be expanded as follows, to include $\widehat{TC}$ thought-choice: S → $\widehat{TC}$ →R. All stimuli upon humans are mediated by the thought-choice and, therefore, the responses are entirely dependent on how the individual chooses to perceive a given stimulus. Because all humans (especially FEEs) can vary their thought-choices at will, there are innumerable responses available to any given stimulus.

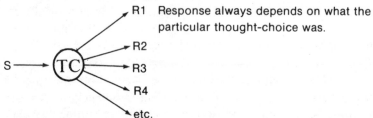

Supposing, for example, the stimulus above was the boss' yelling at you, "You're doing a terrible job in managing this place! Get this place shaped up right away!" One can then mediate this stimulus simply by choosing any one of innumerable thoughts. Here are just a few: (TC) option #1: "Oh my god. I'm really destroyed. He thinks I'm terrible and my work is so important to me. I'm very upset." (TC) option #2: "The boss is a fool. His remarks make him look foolish, not me." (TC) option 3: "The boss is mouthing off again. I can't ever seem to please him. The hell with him. Let me focus on the more interesting aspects of life. I'll pretend that I'm very affected by his criticism, and even look ashamed. But I'll continue enjoying my life." (TC) option #4: "There's some truth to what the boss is saying, even though I don't appreciate his approach. I will tighten up on managing, however. The boss is acting crazy. I won't take his hollering seriously. I'll pay him deference, but I'll quietly make progress my own way."

Try the following. Pause in your reading for a moment, shut your eyes, then think about something very positive, very pleasant. Remember, you can think of anything you want. It's your ultimate freedom. Why not think of something outrageous, wild, fun. You have my permission (and your own) to choose any thought at all, without charge. Perhaps you'll visualize something you never thought of before. Something that was heretofore unthinkable for you. Enjoy.

In offering the above thought-choice suggestion to hundreds of people, I have seen many smiles come to their faces.

Choosing thoughts, even though you may not act them out, can provide you with exciting visceral experiences. Your body, heart, adrenalin, and organs respond according to what you think.

If a tiger were to jump out at you while you were walking through the jungle, your nervous system would leap into action. And if you were walking through the same jungle but only breezes moving the bushes made it seem as though a real tiger was jumping out at you, your body would operate in exactly the same way. Since it is easy to deceive your nervous system, why not regularly deceive it through creative self-deception into having pleasant, healthful, rich experiences whenever you want to? Simply choose pleasant, effective, healthful thoughts as needed.

However, there are, for most of us, those occasions when it is very difficult to choose a useful thought at that very moment we want to. Instead, nasty, self-defeating thoughts sometimes rear up, spoiling our efforts.

For example, just as Lynne, a hypothetical FEE, was about to give a business talk, a self-defeating thought, "Lynne, those people out there who are all staring at you are making you very nervous," came to the foreground of her conscious mind. Naturally, this self-defeating thought seriously impaired Lynne's ability to speak with the ease and spontaneity that she desired.

The more Lynne tried to put this self-defeating thought out of her conscious mind, the more difficult it seemed to become. She then turned to what are called the A, B, C's of choosing thoughts: A = The Aggravation Technique; B = The Branding Tactic; and C = The Closure Process. These are extremely useful when choosing at a conscious level is difficult. These are subconscious choosing methods.

Lynne (A) *aggravated* herself, making her more nervous, but in the process succeeded in putting herself in charge of her tension. Then she (B) *branded* her subconscious with the thought, "Lynne, you'll be calm and collected when you give your speech." Finally, Lynne (C) put *closure* on any unfinished business, her unresolved childhood fears of speaking in public.

If you're unsuccessful at choosing at the straightforward, conscious level, as Lynne was, then use choosing assisted by A, the Aggravation Technique. Then if still deeper help is required, you can go on to B, the Branding Tactic. If still more help is needed, then movement to C, the Closure Process, is in order. You can always use conscious choosing plus the A, B, C's any time at all. Eventually, conscious choosing will be habitual and sufficient.

The Choice Is Always Yours: Use Execupower

Situation: You tried to consciously choose a comforting thought for yourself so that you could fall asleep, but somehow, consciously choosing didn't seem to work for you.

Self-Defeating Thought
I give up. I can't seem to choose a thought. I'll just have to be a victim of whatever my mind pops up with.

Fully Effective Thought
I wasn't able to consciously choose just now. Therefore, I'll resort to the A, B, C's of choosing. That is sure to help.

Roy Peterson, an office manager, was disgusted with his own behavior. "I've got to stop taking out my case of nerves on innocent workers," he muttered to himself. He unsuccessfully tried choosing effective thoughts at the conscious level. He tried thinking, "I feel calm. I won't get upset by minor disturbances." Instead, nerve-wracking thoughts took over. "Feel calm" would certainly be effective if only he could choose it. Because nerve-wracking thoughts dominated his conscious mind, he used the Aggravation Technique, and with great success.

A. The Aggravation Technique is based on the well-established psychological principle of "implosion." Through implosion, the patient makes things worse (aggravating them) before they get better. For example, in order to overcome stuttering, patients are advised to deliberately stutter even more. This puts them in charge, and subsequently, often makes it easier to stop.

Here's precisely how Roy Peterson used the Aggravation Technique to his advantage in overcoming his case of "nerves." The very next time that he felt himself going out of control, he made himself more nervous by choosing nervousness producing thoughts—thoughts such as "I'm carrying too much of a work load. I get no appreciation for all the work I do," and "No one really cares how I feel." These thoughts succeeded in making him more upset than ever. They were effective thoughts, however, for aggravation purposes. The Aggravation Technique placed Roy in charge of his feelings by reminding himself that it was Roy and no one else, not even the circumstances, that was creating his nervousness. He was thus able to start on the road to improvement.

Having succeeded in making himself more nervous, Roy paused and asked himself, "Is this the way I want to feel? More nervous?" Roy, of course, answered himself, "No I don't want to feel more nervous; I want to feel calm. OK, then use Execupower and choose calming thoughts." And to the degree that he chose calming thoughts, he met with success.

The next time you find that you are having trouble consciously choosing, use the Aggravation Technique. It is especially valuable for those occasions when you feel depressed for no identifiable reason and, therefore, find it difficult to locate those self-defeating thoughts that are undoubtedly bringing you down. Deliberately choose thoughts that make you even more depressed; then after you've had enough depression, pause and choose thoughts about sunbathing on a beautiful beach, or having terrific sex with the love of your life, whatever "turns you on" to enjoy life. Your depression will be sure to lift since feeling depressed cannot possibly occur unless you actually have depression producing thoughts preying on you.

B. The Branding Tactic is the second form of choosing that is available to you. The Branding Tactic is a quick and easy self-hypnosis strategy that *brands* effective thoughts deeply into your subconscious.

Green is considered by psychologists to be a very restful color, but you can use any color that you personally find soothing in the Branding Tactic.

Visualize your restful color, perhaps green, in all its natural glory. Put your conscious mind completely at ease by saying "green," visualizing the restful beauty of the color, and suggesting that your whole body relax, from top to bottom. Take a deep breath and let your whole body rest. Then say "green" again. At this point you will bypass your conscious mind by telling yourself "No matter how hard I try, I will not be able to open my eyes." Be sure to go along with this suggestion and do not open your eyes. Otherwise, as you'll see later, you might win the battle, but you'll lose the war. Now say "green" for a third time while suggesting to yourself that all self-defeating thoughts lodged in your subconscious will fade away. Follow this suggestion with the suggestion that you will brand fully effective thoughts deeply into your subconscious. Repeat the effective thoughts (that you've prepared in advance) to yourself, several times if necessary. Now say "green" for the fourth and last time. At this point suggest to yourself that in a few moments you will open your eyes feeling completely refreshed. Then follow your suggestion, open your eyes, and benefit from a reprogrammed subconscious.

Be sure to envision the color green (or whatever color you happen to find most soothing) and imagine it with all its natural restfulness. With your subconscious appropriately branded, it will be much easier for you to choose effective thoughts as needed. Experiment with the Branding Tactic until you've mastered it. You'll find it a very helpful assistance in choosing.

Again, shut your eyes and then say "green." As you say "green," visualize your entire body relaxing from head to toe. Then say "green" to yourself once again, and this time firmly suggest to yourself that "no matter how hard I try, I will not be able to open my eyes." (Of course, you could actually open your eyes if you wanted to, but that would obviously be self-defeating.) It is clearly in your best interest to not open your eyes, since at this point you bypass your conscious mind by going along with your "can't open your eyes" suggestion. Your conscious mind is always the suspicious gatekeeper of your naive subconscious. Your subconscious is always unsuspecting and totally uncritical. Therefore, once you get past the gatekeeper you can suggest practically anything at all to your subconscious and you'll always be given the benefit of the doubt. Therefore, simply go through the motions of trying to open your eyes, but never succeed. Once you do that, you will be in direct contact with your naive subconscious.

As you say "green" for a third time you will have direct access to your subconscious mind. Speak to your subconscious and tell any self-defeating thoughts that bother you to give up. Tell these thoughts that they have no chance to be chosen by you. Let them atrophy. Then visualize a red-hot branding iron with the fully effective thoughts that you want to choose clearly imprinted on it. Brand your subconscious with these effective thoughts. Then say "green" to yourself for the fourth and final time, reminding yourself that in a few moments you will open your eyes refreshed, rested, and quite energized. Now your branded subconscious can readily provide you with those fully effective thoughts that you branded into it.

This Branding Tactic is an easy, quick self-hypnosis, useful to you in numerous ways: to calm yourself down quickly, to overcome such bad habits as smoking, shyness, or overeating, or just to feel more confident and enthusiastic about life. In review:

(1) Green, "I'm completely at ease."
(2) Green, "I can't open my eyes, even though I try."
(3) Green, "Stop choosing the following Self-Defeating Thought(s):"

And, "Choose the following Fully Effective Thoughts:"

---

(4) Green, "In a moment I'll open my eyes, feeling refreshed, relaxed, and energized."

Sam wanted to stop worrying at bedtime so he used a combination of A and B. As soon as Sam put the bed light out he would worry over and over again about reports, deadlines, and the pressures of his job. At first Sam tried the usual method of counting sheep. But nothing, not even a warm shower, seemed to help poor, tired Sam fall asleep. In fact, his efforts to cease worrying at bedtime seemed to have the opposite effect and kept him awake. Sam first used the Aggravation Technique, and forced himself to worry even more. Aggravation clearly put Sam in charge of his bedtime worrying. He then added B, the Branding Tactic, to help him sleep.

As Sam said "green," he felt his entire body relax completely, from top to bottom. The moment he said "green" for the second time, he tried to open his eyes, but to no avail. That's because he reminded himself, "No matter how hard I try, I won't be able to open my eyes." It's important to know that he could actually open his eyes if he really wanted to, but he didn't open them because he felt it was infinitely more important for him to have direct access to his subconscious, the place where his basic worries resided. As he said "green" again, Sam repeatedly chided his subconscious, "Stop bringing all my office worries home at night." He repeated this message several times until it was deeply embedded into his subconscious. Then, still speaking directly to his subconscious, he said, "You will have a series of beautiful scenes from your Vermont vacation appear automatically in your mind in place of the worry." He repeated this calming thought over and over again until it, too, was indelibly branded into his subconscious. Then, with his subconscious branded (reprogrammed) to be fully effective, rather than self-defeating, he said "green" for the final time. Concurrently he said, "I will open my eyes and feel completely at ease and refreshed. I will open my eyes and feel excellent."

In a few moments, Sam slowly opened his eyes. For awhile in bed, he lay there enjoying the pleasant sensation of feeling refreshed. Then suddenly, for no obvious reason, he felt very tired, very sleepy. Sam yawned, rolled over, and in a matter of moments fell off into a deep, sound sleep.

Combining A with B (Aggravation with Branding) created an unbeatable one, two punch and made it possible for Sam to choose effective, sleep producing thoughts. Sam used thought-choice tactics regularly until falling asleep as soon as his head hit the pillow became a matter of habit—a productive habit.

If, after using both A and B methods, Sam were still to find it impossible to fall asleep because of worry, he had one other very powerful strategy remaining at his disposal—C, The Closure Process.

The Closure Process need only be employed when it is extremely difficult to choose effective thoughts over self-defeating ones. The reason it is sometimes so difficult to get nonproductive, self-defeating thoughts out of our heads, even after we've tried and tried is because these self-defeating thoughts are very much connected to some serious unfinished business that we still have to take care of.

Unfinished business, such as not having told a loved one just how much you loved her before she died, or not having told off a colleague who insulted you, or a garage mechanic who failed to repair your car completely after you payed $1400 in charges, can really prey on your mind. Very often we carry a large supply of unfinished business around with us for years and years, some of it from childhood.

Very often our dreams and nightmares help us complete this unfinished business indirectly. This is what therapists often call "working through." Sometimes psychotherapy is needed to "work through" and completely close the doors on unfinished business.

If it's too late to say goodbye or tell someone off because the person in question is no longer available, it's important to find a substitute to "work through" unresolved issues. Therapists know that saying goodbye at the gravesite or telling off an empty chair can often serve as a useful substitute for the real thing. Much unfinished business can be taken care of by yourself using the Closure Process.

The Closure Process involves four distinct stages. These stages do not follow a particular sequence, therefore you can bypass one stage temporarily and then return to it later on. However, eventually all four stages must be completed. When you have completed each stage, you will be free from the pangs of unfinished business, and then you can get on to productive functioning.

The separate stages are *Shock and Disbelief, Wheeling and Dealing, Anger,* and *Disappointment.* When you've completed these four stages, you arrive at Closure, having completed the unfinished business that has been holding you back.

Here's how FEE Don Heath put closure on the unfinished business connected with suddenly being fired from his job for the first time in his life. Don was loyal to his company for twelve years even though his job was very difficult and high pressured.

He gave it the very best he had all the time. "It was the first and only time in my life that I was actually fired from a job. And I took it very badly."

When the president called him on that Monday morning six years ago and announced, "You're fired," Don felt completely numb. He left the office in a daze and wandered around the city that day in total disbelief. He kept repeating to himself, "How unfair. How rotten. This can't really be happening to me. This must be happening to someone else, not me. This must be a dream, a nightmare. Maybe I'll wake up, and it'll be gone." Don obviously was in stage #1, *Shock and Disbelief.* After a time, Don moved beyond shock and entered another stage, *Wheeling and Dealing.* During this stage, he bargained in his mind the various ways that he could win his job back. "I'll work harder; they've got to give me another chance." Once he even fantasized that the president called him into his office and said he made a mistake. But Don came to appreciate that the president was doing exactly what he intended to do. Don was on his knees in his mind's eye. Finally he came to realize *Wheeling and Dealing* was to no avail. It was then that Don Heath became very angry. Stage three is *Anger.* It is always useful and healthy to get angry when you've been hurt, if you are careful not to hurt anyone else in the process. Hitting a pillow or cursing in the confines of your closed car are harmless outlets for anger that can be quite productive.

Therefore, Heath cursed his old boss, the people at that grinding company he gave so much to, and literally anyone at all that he felt had even remotely sabotaged his job success. Once he had enough of anger he moved on to stage four, *Disappointment.* With all the heaviness of heart that goes with being let down, Heath felt a great sadness. This was the effect of his anger turning inward. This heavy-hearted stage is essential if one is to bring unfinished psychological business to completion. After a short, intense period of depression, Heath finally arrived at closure of the wound he experienced by being summarily fired. Now, at closure, he was able to accept the reality of his actually being fired without continued rancor or venom. Eventually, with perspective, Heath said, "It's almost as if the firing was of someone else. I can finally accept the fact that it really happened to me. It happened six year ago and although I haven't forgotten, I certainly have forgiven. I can't forget, but I can always forgive. My philosophy is to take the flames from the past and forget the ashes." He had arrived at full closure on a bad experience.

If Don Heath had not resolved this unfinished psychological business, it would still be preying on his mind and would make it extremely difficult for him to enjoy his present successes. Closure always frees you to get on with the pleasures of living.

Therefore, the next time you are unsuccessful in consciously choosing, use the A, B, C assists. Use them, don't just dream about using them or merely try to choose thoughts that work; actually choose them.

Segment 4. "Fully Effective Thoughts"

If a thought works toward your attaining "one of the most satisfying personal and professional lives ever," then that thought is classified as "fully effective." If it doesn't lead toward that outcome, then it is "self-defeating." However, it is important to note that thoughts that prove effective for one person may not work at all for another.

Recently, a woman who had heard me speak on the values of effective thinking said to me, "Dr. Kushel, I tried choosing an effective thought, but it didn't work for me. How come?" I said, "An effective thought should always work if you choose it correctly." "Well," she said, "I'm on a diet and I've been trying to keep myself from eating certain fattening foods. So just as I was about to eat a big piece of chocolate cake, I employed your effective thought system. I paused and then chose a fully effective thought just as you said to do. But Dr. Kushel your method just didn't work. I ate the chocolate cake anyhow—all of it!"

I then explained to her that there is proof that the method definitely works since FEEs successfully employ it all the time, but that obviously the thoughts she chose were not at all effective. "You owe it to yourself," I said, "to find out the specific thoughts that will work for you. No one, other than you, can be the final judge of that." I then helped her figure out the many effective thoughts that were available to her, thoughts geared to her own, special orientation to life.

Eventually, with some genuine effort on her part, she settled on dozens of them, some of which were quite peculiar. She stopped herself from eating chocolate by imagining vinegar being mixed with it. This worked beautifully for her, to sour her taste for chocolate. But for someone else, quite a different line of thinking might prove more effective.

The Choice Is Always Yours: Use Execupower

Situation: You start believing that effective thoughts don't work for you.

Self-Defeating Thought	Fully Effective Thought
This so-called effective thought choice might work for FEEs but it doesn't work for me.	If a thought I choose doesn't work, then obviously that thought wasn't effective. By definition, "effective" means thoughts that work for me. I'd better go back to the drawing board and design some thoughts that really work for me!

There are fully effective thoughts to be chosen in any given situation whatsoever: if you're suddenly fired from a job, if illness or injury strikes without warning, even if you suffer the loss of a loved one. Of course, the challenge to create effective thoughts in some situations is greater than in others, but no less possible. The method always works without fail. All you have to do is use it. All diets work. The trick is to stay on one.

Effective thinking always translates into effective action. The golfer, below, chooses a thought that creates a feeling of inner calm. This calm helps the golfer concentrate fully on the ball, then act in accordance with his thoughts. If the ball goes into the cup, his thinking was effective. If it doesn't go in, it was not effective. Fully effective thoughts must always produce the desired results, or else the thoughts were not really "effective," by definition.

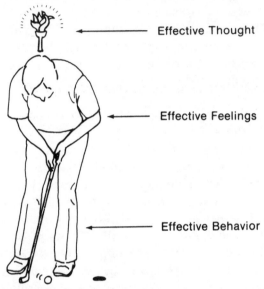

Effective Thought

Effective Feelings

Effective Behavior

There are some thoughts which may not appear to be self-defeating at first glance, but which over the long run reveal themselves as such. For example, be careful to avoid *"I'm"* statements, unless they are of a positive nature. It will serve you poorly, for example, to say: "I'm a nervous person. I'm a worrier. I'm a loser." Or "I'm a victim."

Since these projections become self-fulfilling prophecies, negative *"I'm thoughts"* will only work against you. It's more effective to say *"I'm* bound to be doing better," or *"I'm* a winner," if you want to use self-fulfilling prophecies to your personal advantage.

Also avoid using the word "try" in any promises that you make. Use in their place *"I will"* statements. "I'll try" gives you a ready out, an excuse for not succeeding before you even start. But a firm "I will" indicates a solid commitment. "I will" shows others (and yourself) that you really mean to succeed.

FEEs also always avoid blaming others. They realize that blaming others is usually self-defeating, even if some criticism of others is warranted. Since you, alone, are totally responsible for all of your thoughts, feelings, and behavior, accepting blame puts you in full charge of yourself.

Also, FEEs avoid guilt-producing "shoulds" and "oughts" in their private thinking. Instead of saying "I should" they ask themselves, "Who, if anybody, says I should?" Then they ask themselves, "Where, indeed, does that individual get the authority over me to insist that I should? The only 'should' that I have is to have as satisfying a life as possible in the limited time I have remaining on this planet, and never at anyone else's expense."

FEEs are also wary of *idealistic* positive thinking. They use *realistic* positive thinking, the kind of positive thinking that is based on reality. For example, if a friend of yours has a strange growth in his stomach, treating it with idealistically positive thoughts would be as follows: "Every day in every way, I'm getting better and better." But an FEE would be much more realistic: "I've got a growth that needs to be checked by a physician. Then after the checkup, I'll work it positive from there."

Charlie says to Fred, a confirmed idealistically positive thinker, "Say Fred, you ought to pull the shades down in your house. I saw you there last night with your wife, kissing and hugging, kissing and hugging." "Ha, ha, ha," laughs Fred in return, "Charlie, the joke's on you. Why I wasn't even home last night!"

FEEs believe that it is extremely important to be very precise in the use of words. A man searched far and wide for a physician to "castrate" him, but all the physicians that he approached refused to perform such a nasty operation. Finally he found one doctor who was willing to castrate him. The morning after, the newly castrated man was moaning and groaning in great pain. The patient in the bed next to him had obviously been operated on also. "What kind of operation did you have?" the newly castrated man asked. "Oh," came the reply, "yesterday I was circumsized." "Oh, my god," said the castrated man, *"Circumsized!* That's the word I meant!" Poor soul. He'd now be sure to tell you how important precision in the use of a single word can sometimes be.

Fully Effective Thinking leaves relatively little to chance when it comes to communication. Clear communication with others is extremely important, as in the above instance. Clear communication with oneself is imperative.

Again, the Execupower Principle is **"Whenever necessary/ pause/then choose/fully effective thoughts."** Knowing all about it is one thing. But putting it into practice is what really counts. There's an old Chinese proverb: "I see, and I find interesting. I read, and I find fascinating. But I *do,* and I *understand.*"

Execupower Rehearsals

What are some fully effective thoughts that can be helpful in each of the following situations?

1. You find a large rip in your trousers, just as you are about to enter a client's office.
2. A business prospect has kept you waiting over an hour for your appointment with him.
3. The presentation that you just gave was rated "awful" by the persons that heard it.
4. While you're waiting in a long line at the bank, the clerks seem to take an extended break. This is sure to make you late for your next appointment.
5. Business is very bad. You're becoming quite frightened over the possibility that you might go broke and get even deeper in debt.
6. Your house was robbed and many of your most treasured possessions have been taken.

FEEs always attack difficulties by tackling them from two directions at the very same time—internally and externally. They attack the disturbing issue *attitudinally* with effective thoughts and at the same time *practically* with concrete actions and steps. More specifically, while they apply the Execupower Principle to choose those thoughts that will place them in an optimal frame of mind, they concurrently take whatever practical measures necessary to ease or eliminate the upsetting situation.

The following four-step worksheet is designed to help you plan your approach to any real life situation that you currently find upsetting. What you already know about Execupower can help you immediately. And by the time you finish this program, you'll be able to deal effectively with any untoward situation whatsoever.

The Execupower Worksheet

(1) Briefly describe the disturbing condition that currently concerns you.

_____

_____

(2) What practical external steps can you take to ameliorate or remedy the situation?

_____

_____

(3) What Fully Effective Thoughts can best serve you in view of the prevailing situation?

_____

_____

(4) What Self-Defeating Thoughts are you having that need to be quelled?

_____

_____

_____

Remember to use the A, B, Cs of choosing whenever you need additional help in choosing Fully Effective Thoughts over Self-Defeating ones. Then put the Execupower Principle into regular action, attacking the situation both attitudinally and practically.

The six chapters that immediately follow explain everything that you need to know about the six *practices* common to all FEEs. It is important to note that each of these practices is characterized by the different single Fully Effective Thought that I've placed at the head of each of the next six chapters. Once you've learned all about the FEEs' practice in each chapter, all you'll need to do is to repeat the Fully Effective Thought that heads the chapter; then the scores of additional Fully Effective Thoughts that fall under the heading thought will come to mind. Choose Fully Effective Thoughts regularly and you will be virtually guaranteed your own high level of personal and professional success.

5

THE REALITY PRACTICE

Fully Effective Thought #1: "Be Realistic, Not Merely Reasonable."

FEEs find it important to temper their high expectations with realistic thinking, since this world is often not as idealistic as they would like it to be. FEE Matt Renolds: "This world as it is presently constituted is not a particularly reasonable place. If it were a reasonable place, it certainly would be a better place. But as nearly everybody who's been around knows, this world of ours has some very inhuman and peculiar values."

FEEs consistently separated their realistic expectations from those that were merely reasonable. "It is reasonable," FEE Max Vogel said, "to assume that I will be very much appreciated by this company for many years to come based on all my good works and the recognition bestowed on me over the past seven years. But I know enough about life to realize that that's just not very realistic. That's just not the way business always works. Look, I understand that this company really loves me right now. I'm perceived as doing an excellent job. Sure, I enjoy being so highly regarded by those in power. However, as you know, times inevitably change. It's not only conceivable, it's quite probable that one of these days some new, young, fast-tracking hotshot in this organization will be looking my way with a jaundiced eye and say, 'Well, old-timer, what have you done for us lately?' and point, not so politely, to the door. If that time should ever come, I want you to know that I'll be completely ready to handle it. In fact, I'm prepared now because I've always been very realistic, not only about others, but realistic about myself.

"I'm even prepared to face the hard facts with my wife. Let me tell you about her while I'm at it. It's the same principle. My wife is a very warm, sweet, loving person. That's due in part to the fact that I'm warm and loving with her too. I work hard. I'm faithful, warm, and loving. But I damn well know if I were to change my loving ways there would eventually be a corresponding change in the way that she feels about me. That, I'm afraid, is the way life works. That's reality.

"I've come to terms with the fact that there really is no such thing as a free lunch. In this world, it's strictly value given for value received. Let me tell you, if you don't already know it, life can be tough in the big city."

The Choice Is Always Yours: Use Execupower

Situation: You're torn between pressures at work and pressures at home. You would like to satisfy everyone, including yourself.

Self-Defeating Thought	Fully Effective Thought
All relationships are equal. I'll	I have a pecking order of

(Self-Defeating Thought)	*(Fully Effective Thought)*
spread myself equally (and thin).	relationships, and my family and I need to have a long talk so that we can agree on what has priority—and consider the pros and cons of each.

FEE Loretta Reese is a realist too. "I'm obviously the dreamer type. But I learned long ago to temper my dreams with reality. I think of myself now as a down-to-earth dreamer."

FEE Tom Bennett said that his realistic outlook was the basis for his exuberance for life. "Happiness, as I see it, is doing better than you expected. And since I generally do a hell of a lot better than I expected, I'm pretty happy. That's my secret way of being such an 'up' person and probably one reason why I tend to have so much energy."

Limiting the extent that you are jarred by hurts and disappointments can improve the quality of your life. Since living a satisfying personal and professional life is a deeply ingrained habit for FEEs, this way of looking at things becomes a pattern and a lifestyle. Consider choosing thoughts for yourself that are absolutely realistic the next time you sense that you are being primed for disappointment by a set of external conditions that are not under control.

The Choice Is Always Yours: Use Execupower

Situation: You didn't get that prestigious assignment that you wanted and felt that you were entitled to by virtue of your senior status with the company. This seems to be the handwriting on the wall, that you've gone about as far as you can expect to go with this organization.

Self-Defeating Thought	**Fully Effective Thought**
I'm hurt. I really thought that this company appreciated my	It only hurts for a while. Sure, all my good works might have

(*Self-Defeating Thought*)
good works on its behalf. How could I have been so wrong?

(*Fully Effective Thought*)
been rewarded in the past by the hierarchy here. But I learned long ago not to bank totally on the company for my continued success. I did most of my "good works" primarily because I enjoyed doing them, not because of the wonderful rewards I could always expect in return. However, one small point: in this instance, since I do have seniority, I believe I have a strong case that I will diligently press. Facts are facts, and the company will have to deal with the facts head on, just as I do. Meanwhile, I'd better dust off my resume.

Every day there are examples of unkind persons who get marvelous breaks, and marvelously decent people who are cruelly treated. Every day, some company grinds up a devoted, hard-working employee. Every day, there are newspaper accounts of war, childbeating, rape, molestations, robberies, and disease, as well as reports of natural disasters such as earthquakes, floods and hurricanes. Each day claims its share of innocent victims.

But for the most part, in spite of all the bad news, most of what happens every day is overwhelmingly positive. Every day, someone reaches a high point in his life and for many, especially those who are fully effective, there is a constant, gentle, sometimes even idyllic flow toward a very satisfying life. FEEs sustain their easy movement through rough seas, contrary to the methods of popular "happy-think" advocates, not by happy-think or the simplistic power of idealistic positive thinking. How can one be happy when he knows that two-thirds of the world's population goes to bed hungry every night? They enjoy their lives by facing reality head on, and then working it positive from there.

FEEs appreciate that it is neither realistic nor effective to expect a very high degree of reasonability on the job, at home, or even at play. Being realistic, however, does not mean that they are being negative. For example, it might at first glance seem naive to assume that a salesman will make that big sale on his very first try. But if a careful analysis of his skills and his track record indicated that he was extremely talented, then such an optimistic prediction can also be quite realistic. Realism, therefore, is not the same as negativism. However, more often than not most salesmen will not make a sale to each and every one of the ten prospects that he calls on in a given day. Reality might suggest that he can expect to make only one sale for every ten sales talks that he delivers. Realistic expectations always require a careful analysis of the actual probabilities in a given situation.

Most effective salesmen, in order to minimize wear and tear on their psyche and stomach, prepare themselves in advance for possible rejections. Armed with realistic expectations, the effective salesman will make his sales talks confidently, comforted by knowing full well that when the inevitable rejection comes, he will ease through the day successfully, since he has prepared himself to handle rejection in advance.

In 1982, thousands of Brazilian soccer fans were badly victimized by a terrible disappointment. Brazil was considered the overwhelming favorite to win the World Cup. Most Brazilians were led to expect that their team would win the cup, hands down. This was only "reasonable" since Brazil's team had by far the best record compared to its competition. But realistically, soccer is an exciting game, capable of generating some very surprising upsets.

As it happened, Brazil was taken totally by surprise and beaten by Italy in the finals. In Rio, three persons killed themselves immediately after the upset loss, and five others died from shock. In San Paulo, Brazil, nine suicide attempts took place shortly after the upset occurred. Hospitals all over Brazil that day reported a vast increase in the number of patients requiring treatment for shock and trauma.

This dramatic example illustrates how unrealistic, yet quite "reasonable" expectations can do genuine harm. Realistic, not reasonable expectations would have undoubtedly saved many lives and prevented most of the needless suffering that so many Brazilians brought on themselves that day. Tempering their optimism with reality, Brazilians who thought "It's possible to lose, and if we do, I'll definitely be able to handle it. It's not the end of the world," were obviously much better off than those who suffered needlessly.

In addition to having expectations that are realistic, FEEs also make certain that their expectations are quite accurate. This accuracy results from their use of sound critical thinking skills. Accordingly, FEEs are rarely prey to the various charlatans, crooks, propagandists, and manipulators who thrive on the innocent and naive. FEEs are not taken in by "sloganeering," "glittering generalities," "form over substance illusions," or other propaganda traps that take in so many others. FEE Max Vogel appreciates that *"figures* may not lie, but liars can certainly *figure."* Expert at detecting nonsense, FEEs readily see through the false promise of easy cures and fast buck schemes. They are rarely misled by those few dishonest persons who want to mislead in all fields, including medicine, education, law, psychiatry, politics, business, advertising, and even religion.

FEE Ed Hauser: "I'm known around here as 'old hard ass.' And the description fits. It's exactly what I want to project, and, in some ways, that's the way I might be, though I like to think of myself as essentially warm and decent. Look, if one of my workers shows me that he's capable by virtue of his track record, then I'll give him all the rope he needs to get the job done. But I offer no blind faith and I have no false hopes. What I want is evidence."

However, FEEs are not cynics, but instead are skeptics, very healthy skeptics. They readily differentiate between the baby and the bath water, and they take pains to remove the baby before tossing out the bath water. They are expert at knowing just when to keep their guard up, and also just when to let it down entirely to relax and enjoy. While appropriately defended in danger zones, an FEE rests fully and completely in the company of true friends.

The FEE's precision of thought, his ability to differentiate and separate affords him the opportunity to concentrate totally on the job at hand, rather than be ineffectually preoccupied. Accordingly, you can usually rely on the FEE to give total attention to the person who is sharing with him at the conference table, or count on him to listen intensely to his spouse, children, and friends. Because FEEs readily block out all distractions and focus entirely on where they are, you can ask any FEE figuratively, "Where are you?" and his answer will be "here." Ask him the time and the answer will always be "now." FEEs have as their policy, to focus primarily on "heres and nows" as needed. FEE Matt Renolds: "I always take the flames from the past and forget the ashes."

Having mastered the art of "compartmentalization," FEEs figuratively place all distractions into tiny little boxes, each irrelevancy in its own particular box. Then when an appropriate time comes to give their attention to what is in a particular box, they give that issue its full quota of their considerable energies and talents. In essence, the FEE says to distractions, "Line up as if you're at the supermarket delicatessen. Take a number and wait. Then when your number is finally called, you can be certain that you'll get first class attention." To be sure, the FEE ranks all issues according to priority. High priority issues are treated preferentially. Certainly, sorting paper clips deserves less attention than listening to a loved one, for example.

FEEs compartmentalize similarly their personal life issues from professional life issues. FEEs make clear distinctions whenever necessary between the two. FEE Loretta Reese: "I used to bring my job problems home with me. I'd be preoccupied with my problems at work, even when in bed with my husband. Honestly, I find my work extremely fascinating. Naturally Paul really got turned off when I was always talking about business in bed. In fact, it had a very bad effect on him. For a while, it seemed as if he was becoming impotent. But of course, Paul can be fascinating too—if I give him half a chance. Paul is a great guy, but he is in the retail clothing business, and his work really bores me. However, he's very sensuous in bed. I decided to concentrate totally on Paul when I was with him and, sure enough, after a while he began to perk up. All Paul really wanted to know was that I genuinely cared for him. I've learned not to mix much of my personal life with my professional life unless it makes some sense. And often it doesn't.

"Paul and I have got a whole lot of other things to enjoy when we're together. We both love music, talking about philosophy and ideas, and especially having great sex with each other. Our relationship is first rate. My life has been excellent, ever since I decided to separate my personal life from my job."

FEEs compartmentalize and differentiate not only aspects of their work life and personal life, but also, as noted earlier, "positive thinking" from "effective thinking," "preferences" from "needs," being "cynical" from being "skeptical," and, of course, having "realistic expectations" from having "reasonable expectations." A slight difference in the choice of a word can have a major effect in terms of outcome. As you will see later, FEEs also take pains to distinguish between "eustress" and "distress," between "influence of others," and "control of others," and between "playing a role," and "being a role." Subtle differences such as these can have a significant effect on outcome.

We have expectations about almost everything: getting on an airplane (expecting that it will take off and land safely), ordering dinner in a restaurant (expecting decent service and good food), and driving your car (that the brakes will work and the tires will not blow out).

If you were driving your car through a city and came to a green light at a busy and dangerous intersection, it would be reasonable to expect that the cars coming from other directions into this dangerous intersection would obey the red stop signals that they faced. Realistically, however, you probably know that not all drivers consistently obey traffic signals, and that traffic signals sometimes fail mechanically. Doesn't sheer prudence suggest that it's wise for you to temper your reasonable expectations with realistic caution? Obviously it is prudent to ease up on the gas at dangerous intersections, even when you have the green light. It's undoubtedly much safer to drive defensively. Hence, by appropriately tempering your reasonable expectations with realistic ones, you wisely exercise due caution.

FEEs similarly temper their expectations about prospects for a pay raise, stock market trends, health matters, and the integrity of lawyers, accountants, physicians, and mechanics. They intelligently temper what they can honestly expect from their children during their declining years. Interestingly, however, most FEEs do not show on the surface how realistic they really are. In fact, some appear as indefatigable optimists.

FEE Kevin Blake: "If I were to really have let my secretary know what I thought of her the first week she worked for me, she would have been a nervous wreck. I actually pretended that I had unlimited confidence in her abilities, even though she made dozens of stupid mistakes that first week. Pretending that I believed in her has worked out very well in the long run. Sure, pretending was a bit deceitful, but that kind of pretending hurts no one. In fact, now that she's doing so very well, I'm planning to give her a raise. She's infinitely better than I first expected. Frankly, it's been a joy having her prove me wrong, both me and my realistic expectations."

Projecting optimistic expectations to others often has positive effects, but even so, FEEs keep their realistic expectations on ready reserve, just in case. FEE Bob Rosenberg: "Realistic expectations are like savings in the bank, damn nice to fall back on, if need be."

FEEs tend to be humanistic, warm, people-oriented persons, rather than the cold-blooded Machiavellian types you might think of when you think of realistic persons. That's because FEEs do not see, as Machiavelli did, the meaning of life as cold and empty. Whenever circumstances require an FEE to make a choice between a humanitarian process or coldly productive ends, the FEE always opts for the humanistic way. FEE Jack Evans: "The end never justifies the means. In fact, there is no such thing as ends, only means. I will only do what I have to do, if I will not have to compromise my fundamental sense of decency. I don't intend to leave this planet worse off for my being here." FEEs always stick to their principles, though their principles may be few.

FEE Vera Jennings: "Whenever it comes to my choosing between a principle or making a buck, I always take the principle. You see, I can always make another buck, but I can never get another principle."

Even the FEEs who were employed by companies that had military clients were quick to rationalize that defense work may very well add to the common good in that a good defense so often saves lives in a world that is overresponsive to power and might.

For many persons less effective than FEEs, there is a tendency to resist facing the facts of life as they are. As infants, most of us enjoyed the beauty and joy of idealism, since such idealism kept us safely tucked away from reality. There is, for many, a deep seated resistance to leaving childhood idealism and fantasy behind. Many erroneously hypothesize that growing up will only lead to an adult life that is barren of fun, joy, and freedom. FEEs, however, realize that being mature can be very exciting, especially with all the freedom and power that comes from taking total responsibility. Execupower permits them to live very exciting, meaningful lives that are infinitely richer than the dreams they had as children.

In order to maintain their pleasurable lives at an even keel, FEEs use still another technique called "Mourning in Advance." Mourning in Advance is really arriving at closure before the upsetting condition takes place. It works best in dealing with three extremely harsh realities that all of us will ultimately face: death, unfairness, and loneliness.

By mourning in advance you actually mourn over the demise of certain pleasing illusions that are unfortunately destined to be proven untrue.

FEE Dick Barnes: "My father had been very sick for seven years. After the first four years, the doctors told us his illness was definitely terminal, that it was just a matter of time. However, his eventual passing was a long and painful process. It took three years. I hated to see him suffer so much. I cried many nights before he died. Then last year when he finally passed away, need I tell you I saw his death as a great blessing. There were no tears from me at his funeral. I was all cried out years before. Sure, I loved my father very much and at first I felt guilty because I did not cry at his funeral. But later I came to understand that I had already mourned for his death long before it happened."

FEEs mourned in advance for the loss of certain childhood illusions about being immortal, about life being just and fair, and about being together with others just like themselves.

Often we must be hurt badly by difficult contacts with reality over and over again before we finally accept certain realities as facts. Little by little, our encounters with harsh realities chip away at our idealism, leaving many persons battered, defenseless, and feeling defeated. Many persons become embittered and cynical. But FEEs, largely because they have mourned in advance for these more difficult aspects of life, tend to remain as enthusiastic, positive, and vital as they were as children who are quite un- daunted even in the face of realities that often tear others apart. FEEs accept life for what it is, not for what it ought to be; they face life's difficult realities directly, do what they can about them, and then move forward affirmatively from that point on.

FEE Larry Owens described how mourning works: "What I do is to go (figuratively) into the closet for three days and three nights and cry continuously for the fact that life is unfair. I cry my heart out that having to work so damned hard is terribly unfair, that some people I know who least deserve it get all the breaks. I cry for the fact that so many of my hard efforts for this company often go unnoticed and unappreciated, that no one here seems to appreciate all that I do. I cry my lungs out for all this until I've filled a gallon bucket with my tears. Remember, I do this all in the closet, so to speak, where no one can see it. Then I cover the bucket of tears with plastic wrap so that none of the tears will evaporate. I always keep this bucket of tears secretly stashed away in my closet. Then whenever I get treated unfairly, as I inevitably do from time to time, life being what it is, I simply go to my imaginary bucket of tears in the closet, take the ladle, and dump a ladleful of my tears on the closet floor. And as I do that, I say to myself, 'Herb, you've already cried for that, get on with it.' And then I get on as ever with the business of the day. Why interrupt my limited life for an injustice that I've already cried for?"

Mourning in advance requires that you move into the closure process (Chapter 4) even before you've been badly hurt. You go through shock and denial, wheeling and dealing, anger, disappointment, and arrive at closure well in advance of the incident. When all of these important stages are completed, you are freed in advance of all the pain and anguish that you are bound to experience when the painful event actually takes place.

Herb Ditton's mourning makes it unnecessary for him to be set back each time he is treated badly by life. All FEEs use this trick of mourning to sustain their easy, uninterrupted flow toward their primary goal, a very satisfying life.

Clearly, it is neither necessary nor possible to mourn in advance for everything unfortunate that can possibly happen. However, three harsh realities, your own death, injustice, and some loneliness are absolutely unavoidable. These three realities will surely affect every person currently alive. Although it is possible (though unlikely) that there might someday be a tax repeal, there will never be a repeal of death, unfairness, and loneliness.

Why not choose to live a *F-U-L* life, rather than a *FOOL's* life? *F* stands for the fact that life is *F*inite. *U* stands for the fact that life is essentially *U*nfair. And of course, *L* stands for Loneliness. Live a *F-U-L* life, rather than a *FOOL's* life!

FEEs have mourned in advance for the inescapability of their own death, with thoughts like, "One life per person. Life is far too short. The problem with life insurance is that we either live too long or die too soon. The past is gone forever, subject only to the distortions of selective retention. All my material possessions are really rented; when I die I will not be able to take any of them with me. I've got a retirement attitude now, since my future retirement isn't guaranteed. Even my gravestone, even all those who once knew me will be gone in a few hundred years. I'm on my very short vacation from eternity." All of these statements reflect the FEE's acceptance of his own eventual demise. But before we discuss the inevitability of your own demise any further, let's examine another harsh reality—that of injustice.

Here are some FEE statements that reflect an awareness of the absence of absolute justice: FEE Ted Rogers: "Talent always seems to come like bananas, in bunches. It's unfair, but the bright girl is also probably the most talented. If she's a great dancer, she can also probably sing. It's damned right unfair. But, still, that's the way it is." FEE Matt Renolds: "Some really rotten people do very well and some very wonderful people get the shaft regularly. I see it in this business all the time." FEE Vera Jennings: "All relationships are conditional, value given for value received." FEE Bob Rosenberg: "I've learned to edit my life, since I realize I cannot possibly have it all. It's a shame, but true." FEE Dick Barnes: "I've come to accept that even my children may not honor me in my old age." FEE Larry Burns: "Very few people really listen and care for me strictly on my own terms." FEE Ed Hawser: "Most organizations are probably 'people grinders,' even this one." These thoughts about the unfairness of life were thoroughly mourned for in advance by FEEs to the point of closure. These truths no longer unduly upset FEEs. Each of their statements are food for fully effective thoughts.

FEEs also mourn for the reality that there is a basic loneliness inherent in human existence. "When I was born," they believe, "the mold was broken and thrown away. There never was a person just exactly like me in the history of mankind, and there will never be one exactly like me again. I am one of a kind. No cloning of me is possible. Unfortunately, no matter how close others can get to me there is still part of me that is very much alone. I was born alone and I will inevitably die alone. There is no one alive who will be able to give me another breath after I take my last one. I'll be taking my last breath all alone. Out of my acceptance of loneliness I have had to come to terms with the fact that I am a very special person who has special unique purposes for living."

Now that you're briefly familiar with the FEEs basic attitude toward a F-U-L life, let's discuss F-U-L more completely. Remember, everything that we discuss can be used by you, as needed, should you need effective thoughts about reality in your own life.

Your life is definitely *finite*. Many persons, as children, believed that their life would somehow go on indefinitely, that they possessed some special magical quality that would deliver them from death.

Hugh Jennings, a less than fully effective executive, came to me for counseling. Suddenly, at middle age, he was struck with the reality that he was not immortal and he wanted it all before he died. "I think I'm slowly going out of my mind," Jennings confided. "Here I am, a supposedly happily married man, with a lovely wife and three gorgeous kids—and I'm involved in this wretched love affair on the side. It's driving me bananas. Yesterday, I pulled my car over to the side of the road. My heart was aching and I started to cry. Before I knew it, I was crying out 'I want it all! I want it all!' It's a good thing the car windows were closed."

Wanting it all in one's lifetime is a reasonable but infantile desire. FEEs have learned to accept the reality of not having it all. They never try to get it all, ruining whatever they have, and ending up with nothing worthwhile.

FEE Herb Ditton: "When I was a little boy, I used to think that I had all the time in the world. I just couldn't imagine that this world could ever get along without me. But as an adult I realize that was just a childhood fantasy. Unfortunately my life, just like everybody else's, is definitely going to end. It's going to probably be sooner than I want it to be. Imagine, someday the sun will rise signaling another bright new day and I won't be here to enjoy it.

"Somehow when I was a kid, I always figured that at the last minute there would be a reprieve from somewhere, a special 'exemption from death' certificate of some kind. But I've come to terms with the fact that I'm mortal just like everyone else. Surprisingly, when I finally completely accepted the fact that my death was inevitable, I really started to live. I figure that since time is running out, I'd better get to enjoying my life while there's still time. But since I can't do everything, I've concentrated on quality rather than quantity."

When a person believes that he has unlimited time, he tends to waste it. Students often put off studying for tests until the eleventh hour, then cram. FEEs know they have a deadline but they don't cram. They live gentle, flowing lives, while still aware that their time is running out. Although they know that there are no special 'exemption from death' certificates, they persist in living high quality, satisfying lives, focusing on quality rather than quantity. They know that it is impossible to have it all, if "all" means doing everything with little regard for the consequences of one's actions.

Last June during an Execupower Program that I was conducting, a participant commented, "Dr. Kushel, when you described how FEEs have come to terms with the fact that their life was finite, you reminded me of something. I am a Buddhist and we Buddhists believe that when a person is born, it is written in the heavens that he has only so many breaths. Each person is given a certain number of breaths, and no more." She then added wryly, "That's why we Buddhists breathe very, very slowly!" Although none of the FEEs in my sample happened to be Buddhists, all of them believed that there were only a limited number of moments designated to compose their lifetime.

Jastrow, the noted space scientist, is said to have estimated that this planet is already about seven billion years old. He also estimated that there are an additional 14 billion years left before the earth finally moves so close to the sun that it boils over, or so far away that it turns into a solid ball of ice. Either way it'll certainly be the end of this planet as we know it.

An effective way to look at this is to consider that those of us alive today have already spent about seven billion years in eternity. Then we suddenly popped into life for about three score and ten years. Clearly, our short time alive is very limited; viewed from the perspective of eternity, it's a mere drop in the proverbial bucket. When you consider that all of us who are alive today are destined to spend 14 more billion years in eternity after our death, the short time we have remaining to live is very short indeed.

The remaining 20 minutes or 20 years that you've still got ahead of you is the remainder of a very, very short vacation from eternity. FEEs always look at their life as a short vacation from eternity. They have a personal mandate to enjoy life, even if things go sour, their spouse divorces them, the stock market dips, or they lose their jobs. They simply remind themselves emphatically that they are on vacation and as FEE Ted Barton said, "I'm not spending my limited time alive fighting for deck chairs on the Titanic."

Life can sometimes be very unfair. Sometimes, for example, dreadful things happen to really nice people. Also, it is true that some very indecent persons sometimes manage to do very well, to get rich, have good luck, and even get top jobs. But FEEs can accept these realities. FEE Neil Evans: "As badly as I seem to be doing sometimes, it's likely that someone else is doing much worse and is in fact looking at me with envy." It is true that there is always likely to be someone who is doing better than you are at any given time, but it is equally true that there's likely to be more than a few more who are doing much worse than you are.

FEEs concentrate on and enjoy whatever it is that they currently have, avoiding as many jealous comparisons as possible. Fastidiously applying the Execupower Principle, FEEs choose fully effective thoughts, reminding themselves that justice is a very relative concept. FEEs, recognizing justice as relative, never lose sleep over the fact that they might not get the pay raise that they so reasonably deserve, or that their tax forms were selected for a biased government audit rather than someone else's. Nor do they lament excessively if they get an undeserved traffic summons. It's not that they are passive or disinterested in justice. In fact, to the contrary, they often fight passionately to right an obvious wrong. But they lose no sleep over the reality of injustice. They conserve their emergency energies to wage a good fight when the right time comes, if indeed fighting makes any sense at all.

The late Walter Kauffman, renowned Princeton University scholar, highlighted the relativity of 'absolute justice' in his book, *Without Guilt and Without Justice*. Kauffman pointed out that 'absolute justice' is impossible to measure. Justice, he said, is merely a state of mind. And accordingly, FEEs, as is their policy, choose a state of mind that work favorably for them, in spite of the seeming injustice in a given situation.

The Choice Is Always Yours: Use Execupower

Situation: Your spouse blames you for not doing your fair share in managing the household.

Self-Defeating Thought
How outrageous. How unfair. I'm miserably wronged and I feel victimized.

Fully Effective Thought
Seemingly wronged again. However, there's no such thing as 'absolute justice' and I've already mourned in advance for that fact. Tomorrow I'll say to my spouse, "Let's find a middle ground where both of us can do our share."

FEE Jim Geary: "Even though I can now accept injustice with relative ease, I've still been known to attack a windmill or two in my day. However, I always make it my business to bounce back from upsets very fast."

FEEs also bounce back from the pain they experience when they discover how lonely life can sometimes be. They appreciate that most of the important works of man have come out of man's existential loneliness—great works of art, music, religion, literature, and science. Van Gogh, Beethoven, Edison, Shakespeare, Newton and other geniuses were essentially loners. FEEs have discovered a paradox, that as they welcome loneliness into their life, rather than run away from it, they join company with the family of man. A man in deep pain can readily testify as to what loneliness is. Ask anyone who has experienced suffering, depression, feelings of loss, uncontrollable jealousy, or misery, and he'll tell you all about loneliness. Unfortunately, no one can do your suffering for you. You do it all alone. Therefore, FEEs compassionately reason "If I let some suffering into my life, I'll join the family of man."

David Reisman, mentioned earlier, pointed out that the real danger is not in the acceptance of loneliness but rather the fear of loneliness, "loneliness anxiety."

FEEs apparently have learned to stop fearing loneliness and instead have learned to accept it, or at least to endure it. FEE Ed Hawser: "Anything that I've ever accomplished that was truly important was done alone. It isn't that I prefer working alone, it's just that I seem to accomplish the most alone, especially when it's something complicated, or something requiring original thinking. After I figured out what I had to all by myself, I then took it to the group and became a team player. And, of course, that part is really the most fun. You see, there's one part of me that is really very much alone and private and another part that is very gregarious indeed—an outgoing, people person." Hawser was certainly more than what met my eye initially, appearing social to an extreme.

The irrational fear of loneliness keeps many persons on the run, yet if they permitted themselves to occasionally experience this dreaded demon, they'd find that loneliness isn't all that useless. In fact, loneliness is necessary to help one stop to find out what they really want out of this busy, busy life. While most persons flee from loneliness, FEEs pause, accept, mourn for it, and find closure and inner peace. As they let loneliness into their lives, they face it directly, then move forward enthusiastically from an independent base.

Alone, as we all really are in the final analysis, FEEs appreciate that they are persons with very special and unique purposes. Accordingly, they have little need to play superficial games and busy themselves with artificial busy-work.

When mourning in advance for the loneliness of life, the FEE asks himself, "Do I really want to live my life in spite of my loneliness or do I want to merely suffer?" Of course, the FEE invariably chooses life. Out of this despair, the FEE, in fact, clarifies for himself his own special life purposes. His purposes often include loving and caring for others. FEE Jack Miller: "One of my most important life purposes is to love my wife and kids. And I do, very much. What I like about loving is that loving another person is totally under my own control. I can love anybody I want to even if they don't love me back. I love my family and I love my friends."

FEEs' purposes also usually include making a special contribution to this world. FEEs always make certain that there are sufficient aspects of their professional work that are compatible with their deeper values. For example, if they are in insurance sales, they must truly believe that their product actually helps people if they are to sell it. If in manufacturing, there again they must find aspects of manufacturing that are compatible with their larger life purposes. While some businesses are clearly less humanistic than others, FEEs must always find some aspect of their work that is acceptable to their life goals. Whenever this proves impossible, FEEs quit that line of work and enter a field that is more in keeping with their serious life purposes.

FEE Mike Richards: "I was an engineer when I first started out. I worked for the Army. It wasn't for me. I got out of engineering as soon as I could. It's important for me to believe very much in what I'm doing. Not necessarily every part of what I'm doing, but at least a substantial part."

FEE Dick Barnes on loneliness: "Everything seemed to point to my getting the presidency of my company. I was the most qualified candidate according to everyone in the organization, or at least, so they said to me. The chairman of the board and all his cronies had me believing for years that the big job was automatically going to be mine when it finally opened up. 'We're grooming you, Dick,' they said. But then much to my shock and dismay, suddenly and without warning, they brought in a young guy from the outside. A fast tracker. I couldn't believe it at first. How could they have done this to me? Those bastards. It wasn't not getting the job that hurt the most. What really hurt was the betrayal by those people in the company who I really thought were my friends.

"I was really hurting. My wife tried to console me, and a few friends tried to reach out—but nothing, absolutely nothing, seemed to help. I never felt so desperately alone in my entire life, alone with my own ache. It took a long time, but since then I've learned to accept the fact that as close as some people want to get to me, there's still a part of me that is very much alone. Although

I never got that presidency, I learned plenty about loneliness.

That rejection turned out to be one of the best things that ever happened to me in my entire life. The pain of rejection helped me to grow up, to see life for what it is, and finally to accept it. Life, since then, has become much better for me. A few years later I became president of another company. But that initial rejection was a million dollar course in executive training. Since that time, I've stopped running from loneliness, knowing full well that I can handle it, should it come. And it does. In case you don't know it, it can be quite lonely at the top."

The Choice Is Always Yours: Use Execupower

Situation: A younger, less experienced person gets that big job that you had expected to get for yourself.

Self-Defeating Thought

I dislike this fast tracker who hasn't even paid his dues. This situation makes me furious. This terrible experience really burns me out. I feel awful.

Fully Effective Thought

I might at first resent a fast tracker, but then I pause and look at it more effectively. I wouldn't mind being a fast tracker myself. I remind myself that there is no such thing as absolute justice. Therefore, why should I waste my energy being unnecessarily upset over this? The clock is running out on me and life is too short to suffer. Also, I wish anyone who can get ahead, all the best; it's great to see anybody who can beat the system. More power to him. As for me, I intend to keep moving forward at my own steady pace. I'm like a cork. I always rise to the top, given sufficient time.

FEE Matt Renolds described how an encounter with his own death made him aware of how alone he really was. "My doctor took me into his consultation room and said, 'Matt, I'm sorry to have to tell you this, but the tests are conclusive. You have no more than three months left to live.' His words hit me like a ton of bricks. Talk about feeling *alone*. That was alone! No one, absolutely no one, could console me. I had to console myself, all alone. And I did eventually. I had to come to grips with the fact that I was really going to die in less than ninety days. Then the damned doctor turned out to be wrong. 'It's a miracle' everyone said. Believe me, I don't ask too many questions about it. Anyhow, that was over twelve years ago and right now I couldn't feel better."

Matt explained how this lonely encounter with facing his own death changed his life dramatically. "Until that time, I never really knew what loneliness was. It was then that I first realized that no matter how much others cared for me, absolutely no one but me could possibly live my life for me. I realized then that as close as I could get to another person (and I can get damn close; I love my wife and family), there is still a very important part of me that is very much alone. But since I've come to accept a certain fundamental loneliness, I've stopped running around in wild, frenzied circles. By accepting loneliness, I was able to see for the first time my unique purposes in life. My purposes are first, to enjoy life, second, to be a caring and loving husband, and third, to accomplish certain things professionally. And that's it. Everything else is more or less superficial."

The Choice Is Always Yours: Use Execupower

Situation: A strange lump continues to grow in your stomach. You've had this for some time now.

Self-Defeating Thought	Fully Effective Thought
Every day in every way, I'm getting better and better. No need to get this checked.	I'd better get this checked by a physician and then, no matter what, work it positive from that point on.

Since FEEs have clearly come to terms with their existential aloneness, when they decide to participate on a team, to get married, or to be a good friend to someone, they do so out of preference, rather than out of the fear of being alone.

FEE Phil Roberts: "Every baseball team needs a shortstop, a first baseman, a pitcher, and a catcher. If the shortstop tries to play first base as well as shortstop, he leaves his own position wide open. You can't play every position at once if you're on a team. Since I've accepted the fact that I can't do everything even though I would like to, I've been a better team player. But accepting the fact that I can't do everything, at least in this lifetime, was difficult for me. It made me feel disappointed and alone for a time. But now I can be a good team player, if it takes a team to win ballgames."

FEEs look upon being married, at least in part, as "living alone together with someone very special." Their version of marriage is of two separate, whole individuals combining their unique resources into a winning team. The formula, then, for marriage is not the usual one half person plus another one half person equals one whole marriage ($\frac{1}{2} + \frac{1}{2} = 1$ marriage). Instead, FEEs view marriage as one whole person plus one additional whole person plus one marriage, which adds up to three (1 person + 1 person + 1 marriage = 3). If a person has his or her act together and then joins another in marriage, prospects for a successful marriage are much greater. And those FEEs who were married knew how to make their marriages work.

The Choice Is Always Yours: Use Execupower

Situation: You've been betrayed by a person you thought was a true friend.

Self-Defeating Thought	**Fully Effective Thought**
Betrayal is too painful. That's	All relationships are

(*Self-Defeating Thought*)
it! It's all over between us.

(*Fully Effective Thought*)
conditional, value given for value received. There's a pecking order to relationships. My friend might have let me down in this instance, but there are some aspects of our relationship that are still worthwhile. Although I will not forget betrayal, I can always forgive it.

Following are twenty-two reality thoughts. Ascertain those that are self-defeating from those that are fully effective. Mark FE (Fully Effective) or SD (Self-Defeating) after each statement in accordance with your opinion. (The correct answers are at the end.)

1. "I can always count on _____."
2. "I can count on _____, but only up to a point. All relationships are conditional, value given for value received."
3. "_____ seems to be listening to me, but it's probably only a part of what I'm saying that is likely to be fully understood."
4. "_____ undoubtedly is listening and caring for me on my own terms."
5. "I can face the truth directly. I may not like it. But I can definitely handle it."
6. "I can't bear to face the truth. I prefer it 'sugar-coated.'"
7. "I'm a skeptic."
8. "I'm a cynic."
9. "I've got all kinds of time. I can defer the pleasures of life until after I retire."
10. "My time is definitely running out. I'm on my short vacation from eternity right now!"
11. "Nasty people will definitely get punished."

12. "Nasty people are sometimes not punished. In fact, some-times they do very well. There is no such thing as 'absolute justice,' but I can accept that now that I've mourned in advance."

13. "I'm lonely at a certain level, but I've learned to accept it, even enjoy it. Through loneliness, I clarify my special purposes as a human being."

14. "I refuse to be lonely. I keep very, very busy, avoiding loneliness."

15. "I am totally open in all aspects of my life."

16. "Openness always depends on the conditions. Truth is subjective, relative to the speed of light."

17. "I'm embarrassingly lucky."

18. "The wiser I work, the luckier I get. I make my own breaks."

19. "I edit my life, quality before quantity. I can't do it all. But I know what I really want out of my limited life-span on this planet."

20. "I'm determined to do absolutely everything before I go!"

21. "I'm bound to get a fair shake one way or another, either in this life or the next."

22. "There's no such thing as 'absolute justice.' I can accept that, even as I move effectively toward improving the situa-tion."

The following numbers are Fully Effective Thoughts: 2, 3, 5, 7, 10, 12, 13, 16, 18, 19, 22. The remainder are Self-Defeating.

It is important to know why one thought is fully effective, while another, though similar, might be self-defeating. You might want to review parts of this chapter, if you're unclear. Remember, in the final analysis, a fully effective thought is only one that works for you in a given situation. If any of the thoughts listed here do not work for you, then it would be your task to find or design thoughts that really do work for you. And, of course, always choose thoughts to live a F-U-L life, rather than a FOOL's life.

Pause, then design at least one fully effective thought based on the reality practice for each of the following situations:

(1) You've worked hard to prepare an excellent business meeting. Yet, on the day of the meeting, no one appreciated your efforts.

_____

_____

(2) Your child who is away at college doesn't even bother to write or phone you, unless it's for more money.

_____

_____

(3) Your best friend takes off with the person who you thought loved you more than anyone else in the world.

_____

_____

(4) You get seriously ill.

_____

_____

(5) No one invites you to a gathering, and you feel badly neglected.

_____

_____

Always take self-responsibility, even if at first it seems as though it is the external condition that is causing your upset. Be sure to rephrase any problem in such a manner as to put yourself into the position of responsibility. By placing yourself in charge, you put Execupower into action. Then choose realistic thoughts, rather than merely reasonable thoughts. If necessary, you might even want to draw on your hidden identity to help you deal with certain situations. That's next.

6

THE HIDDEN IDENTITY PRACTICE

Fully Effective Thought #2:
"Use Your Hidden Identity,
Not Your Job Title or Family Role."

All FEEs have a hidden identity, an identity that goes far beyond the various roles that they play at home and at work. This hidden identity is more important to FEEs than their job title, their given name, or even their family role. What is more, the FEEs' hidden identities were attained long before they were so eminently successful at their careers. It seems abundantly clear that this hidden identity was a major force in assisting them to move ahead, professionally and personally.

The most important question that any person can ever seriously ask himself is "Who am I?" The answer, if taken to heart, not only indicates who you are, but also what will become of you. Any prophecy that you make about your future will have a tendency to become the actual scenario for your future. So if you tend to see yourself as a success, successful you will most likely become. If you see yourself as a failure, that is what you will most likely become. Therefore, it isn't very wise to predict that you will become a nervous wreck, for if you do, you will most surely end up just as nervous as you predicted.

It is important to answer the question "Who are you?" as optimistically as possible. Following are five slightly different versions of the "Who are you?" question. Please answer each of these, but be sure to answer each question somewhat differently each time. Avoid responding with such stereotypical answers as your name, your job title, or "I'm me." Be imaginative, creative, and optimistic in your answers, yet be sure to tell exactly who you *really* are, each and every time.

(1) *Who* are you? Answer: I am . . .

_____

_____

(2) Yes, but who are you *really*? (Answer somewhat differently this time and differently each time hereafter.) Answer: I am . . .

_____

_____

(3) Yes, I can appreciate what you've said about above, but actually who are *YOU*? Answer: I am . . .

_____

_____

(4) Yes, but I find that your definition is still quite insufficient. Who *ARE* you? This time pull out all stops. Answer: I am . . .

_____

_____

(5) Yes, but who are you? Try to be very clear and precise. Answer: I am . . .

_____

_____

Most persons who attempt to seriously answer these Who are you? questions are usually less than completely satisfied with their responses. In fact, for the more than ten years that I have conducted this same exercise with hundreds of graduate students at the college where I work, students often approached me nervously and said, "Dr. Kushel, I'm a little bewildered with my answers. I don't feel very comfortable with them." And then they would ask, "How was I supposed to answer?" Eventually I realized that relatively few people really know with absolute certainty who they really are, beyond their limited social and family roles, or their given name. A role is certainly not who you really are. Nor is your true identity limited to your job title, or even your title in the family such as "son," "mother," or "father." Your given name and family roles are not at all of your own choosing. And your job and job titles are far from entirely under your own control.

In order to attain a level of success that approaches the FEEs' three-dimensional success, it is imperative that you define yourself completely on your own terms and in such a way that you program yourself in advance for the success that you are after.

Some years ago it was observed that peoples' ears wiggled ever so slightly when their given name was called. Undoubtedly, if we had tails, our tails would wag also, just like a pup's. Your given name has been bombarded deeply into your subconscious since birth. Your response to hearing your name is a result of systematic conditioning since infancy, but it is certainly far removed from describing who you really are.

Nor is your job title or role in the family a genuine indication of who you really are either. For example, if someone were to see himself primarily as the President of XYZ Company (presuming he actually had such a title), he would be in a precarious psychological position. His job depends on many variables, some of which may be very much out of his control.

Most presidential jobs are not especially secure. They usually depend greatly on sustaining the goodwill of various other persons and on the economy for its stability. The board, the consumer, and the economy really are in charge of who this president is. FEEs never place their identity into such a brittle, dependent arrangement. Who they are is far too important to be totally dependent upon the caprice of others or circumstances beyond their control.

Jack Aldridge expressed his primary identity as being "an excellent father to my daughter." However, when his rambunctious 13-year-old said to nearly everyone, "My father stinks as a father," Jack became confused, torn, and depressed. "After all I've done for that child," he lamented. It eventually dawned on him that if he were to survive with reasonable mental health, he could no longer continue to define himself as a good father to his daughter. "If my daughter sees me as a failure as a father," he said, "there's not all that much I can do about it. I might be able to change a few things, but it's foolish to predicate my entire identity upon what she thinks of me. I'm not really in full charge of what she chooses to think about me. But I am in full charge of what I think about me, and 'great father' isn't who I am anymore."

During the course of my counseling with Jack, he learned to develop for himself an independent "success-oriented" identity. This new identity was not controlled in any way by the capricious perception of another. Jack kept his new identity to himself and he took it very seriously. This new identity of his proved to be much more satisfying than the one based on a family role.

His deeper identity, "Peaceful River," was a self-picture that was fully under Jack's own control. "Peaceful River" was a self-definition that Jack created entirely for himself. "One of the best parts of being 'Peaceful River' is that it can never be spoiled by ordinary reality and certainly my daughter isn't in control of me anymore. Strangely, I've even become a better father according to my daughter. Sometimes I do better by not trying too hard."

All FEEs, I learned, had some kind of backup inner identity for themselves. This identity was kept on ready-reserve to provide them with a vital self-concept as needed, a self-concept that was not in any way subjected to capricious control by others or by outside circumstances. During the course of my interviews with FEEs, I was surprised at the degree that each of them held strongly to an inner vision of self that was profoundly meaningful to them. Very often, I found this inner self-picture was in the form of a metaphor taken from nature or a self-concept with a religious undertone.

The Choice Is Always Yours: Use Execupower

Situation: You find that your present job is in jeopardy.

Self-Defeating Thought	Fully Effective Thought
My job title is the primary indication of who I really am. I'll be ruined if I lose this job.	Who I really am is definitely not predicated upon my job title. I definitely have an inner identity of my own choosing that describes who I really am. I am . . . (inner identity).

FEEs who relied on a spiritual definition of themselves such as "child of God," were not all that different from the others who also had mystical, larger than life self-pictures. Although most FEEs were not religious in the formal sense, each had a strong self-image that was mystical and larger than life.

FEE Kevin Blake: "I often think of myself on this beautiful, secluded beach. I guess, if really put to the test, that's who I really am. This beautiful secluded beach, with the ocean tides, the gorgeous sky, and all that fantastic potential ready to be fulfilled."

During Execupower workshops, I have assisted many participants in the development of a more useful self-image. If you slowly read the following script into a tape recorder, and then listen to the playback, following all instructions carefully, you too can discover such an identity for yourself. As you listen to your own voice, follow each of the suggestions step by step. All pauses are for about six seconds each. Set yourself in a quiet comfortable place, close your eyes, and then take a nice deep, relaxed breath. Begin as follows:

"Imagine that you are in a place of great beauty in your life.

(pause) Imagine all of the sights, smells, tastes, feelings of this place of great beauty that you are visiting in your mind's eye. (pause) This is a place of great beauty. Imagine such a place, now. This place is entirely of your own choosing, a creation of your own mind. (pause) Visualize it clearly. (pause) Now permit yourself to enjoy the beauty of this lovely place in your mind's eye. Now take a long, deep breath, then relax and permit yourself to experience a great deal of inner peace, serenity, and calm. (pause) Enjoy a great sense of inner calm, right now. (pause) Now, see yourself slowly moving easily about this beautiful place of yours. (pause) Visualize a hidden, small, winding path that seems to be leading off to another even more beautiful place in the distance. Feel yourself walking along this pleasant path toward this other even more beautiful place, a place off in the distance. (pause) This other place is a very beautiful, important, and exciting place to head toward. As you glide along the path toward this place, pause to experience the gentle sense of excitement you feel as you move forward with gentle anticipation. Actually feel this gentle flow of excitement in your body. (pause)

"Take a slow, deep, and easy breath. (pause) Be very much aware of what you are experiencing at this very moment. What are you experiencing in your chest? (pause) Your stomach? (pause) Your face? (pause) Now experience it all at once, the combined sense of inner calm (pause), a sense of clear purpose (pause), and currents of gentle excitement and adventure. (pause) Inventory your feelings from top to bottom. (pause) What do you feel right now on your chest? (pause) Your legs? (pause) Your stomach? (pause) Your jaws? (pause) What are you currently feeling? (pause) Give this whole experience, this place, and everything that you are now feeling a name. (pause) Give this experience, this place, this event an interesting name. (pause) Now slowly open your eyes. (pause) You feel completely refreshed and relaxed."

Now let's review the experience you just gave to yourself. Describe the place of great beauty that you visited in your mind's eye. Was there water in this picture? Beach? Sky? Mountains?

Most workshop participants usually imagine combinations of land, sea, and sky. I believe this occurs because land, sea, and sky are basic images that are deeply ingrained into our subconscious. Certainly, the land, sea, and sky will be here long after we are gone.

The place that you imagined was totally a product of your own creativity. The fact is that no other human being has ever seen this place in exactly the same way that you have just imagined it. This experience of yours may very well reflect who you are much more accurately than your given name, the various roles that society has foisted upon you, or other identities you've had in mind over the years.

Consider this self-picture, this experience that you have just created for yourself, as an inner identity that you can use any time you see fit.

FEEs always keep their inner definition on reserve, ready for use whenever needed. They use this backup identity as a means to calm themselves or to improve their senses, life purposes, and meaning. Periodically, all you need to do is recall the good feelings that you experienced as you moved along the path in the picture you've just imagined. Every FEE has the goal of achieving a general sense of inner calm, combined with clarity of personal purpose, and plenty of excitement and adventure.

FEE Jim Geary: "These three qualities—calm, purpose and adventure—are what make my life so satisfying. And the inner picture of myself contains all three of these qualities. It is a constant source of nourishment for me, especially when the pressures of deadlines in this newspaper business start to get to me. I simply bring my inner picture to my conscious mind as often as possible, sometimes two or three times a day, and remind myself that I'm not just boss of this paper, but something much larger than that. This inner picture that I have of myself always puts everything else into perspective."

The FEEs' picture was always composed of three essential elements: inner calm, a sense of purpose, and adventure.

In your own self-picture, the calmness can be found in the beauty and serenity of your special place; adventure occurs as you move along the path, and your purpose is represented as you anticipate an even more beautiful place or experience off in the distance. These three elements are central to every important aspect of life.

For example, the popular game of golf has calm, purpose, and adventure structured into it as follows: one finds calm as he centers on stroking the ball. Purpose is manifested by the goal of aiming the ball toward the hole. Adventure is experienced in risk taking. Who knows for sure just where the ball will ultimately land?

In a broader context, calm, purpose, and adventure are found in relation to the earth as it encircles the sun. The earth spins around its axis, turning round and round. This produces an inner calm, a center. Then as the moon circles around the earth, that agitation produces excitement and adventure. Tides ebb and flow. In addition, the primary purpose of the earth, viewed from the cosmic perspective, is to simply go around the sun. Hence, calm, purpose, and adventure are structured into the earth, sun, and moon.

From a microscopic perspective, calm, purpose, and adventure are also fundamental. The nucleus, with its protons and electrons are miniature replications of the earth, sun, and moon. Again, even under the microscope, the atom has calm, purpose, and adventure structured in it. And of course, the very same three ingredients that FEEs attain by thought-choice—calm, purpose, and adventure—are essential for a satisfying life.

If you can thoroughly program yourself for prosperity, happiness, and pleasure, then such a life can become a reality for you. FEE Matt Renolds: "I'm really 'acting' as if I'm Chairman of the Board of Vulcan Oil. I'm not really Chairman of Vulcan Oil. I'm really Chairman of the Board in Charge of Matt Renolds."

The Choice Is Always Yours: Use Execupower

Situation: You feel guilty that you are not entirely an "organization man."

Self-Defeating Thought
I need "group-think." I'm the consummate organization man. Completely loyal.

Fully Effective Thought
I'm fundamentally a loner, but I can comfortably work well with others. However, I do my most creative work all alone. I easily play the role of the "organization man," but of course, I'm much more than that.

Network TV Producer, FEE Ted Rogers: "Fifteen years ago, I was a detail salesman representing Knoph Pharmaceuticals and I was calling on this very important surgeon in Dallas. This particular doctor was notorious for putting all salesmen down. Just because he was an M.D., he thought he was a cut better than anyone else. I was young then and I was very much intimidated by this physician, especially when he used his complicated med-school jargon.

"Then one day it occurred to me that I was very accomplished in my own right. I happen to have had extensive training in music and was, in my early years, considered to be a very accomplished concert pianist. Although I haven't made my living as a concert artist, I still believe that I have a very special talent, one that is just as important or even more important than being a surgeon. In my view, music is even more exacting and there's never been anything more exciting or worthwhile. Of course, I appreciate that being a surgeon is an accomplishment too.

"However this fellow just didn't know the first thing about my musical talents and accomplishments. All he knew was that I was just a drug detail salesman making a call, trying to sell him something, and that he was so much better than me.

"Whenever I called on him, I always reminded myself that I was very special in my own right. I pointed out to myself that he was no better than me, that he put his pants on the same way that I did, one leg at a time. I figured that I probably was even a little bit sharper and brighter than he was, even though I didn't have

M.D. after my name. It was amazing. After I reminded myself of all these ideas, I felt at least 10 feet tall. I just couldn't be intimidated by anyone. My inner credentials are just terrific.

"It's interesting. After I developed this method, I really began to sell like a dynamo. I was no longer intimidated by anyone, let alone this physician. This technique has been a part of me ever since.

"I privately think of myself as 'The Grand Concert Master!' even though that's not what I do for a living. This attitude that I developed back then has taken me right to the top of the very competitive business of network TV production. Now you must know how competitive the network TV business is. Every day your head is on the chopping block. It's life in the fast lane. If it weren't for my inner picture 'Grand Concert Master' I'd never be able to stay on top. No question about that. I owe my success to that doctor."

The Choice Is Always Yours: Use Execupower

Situation: You have a compelling urge to use your important new job title to impress friends.

Self-Defeating Thought	**Fully Effective Thought**
I'm so very proud of my new job title that I could bust. Who can blame me? Let me share all my joy.	I'm really pleased over my new position, but it's not the end-all. Other people really don't enjoy hearing someone else boast. Calm down. Remind yourself of who you really are.

In naming your inner self, you might consider appropriating a name from one of the greats in history, literature, or the arts. Or you might consider using the title from a motion picture, a book, the name of a ship, or even your favorite vacation retreat. Perhaps the title of the lifeline that you completed in Chapter 3 is suitable. Choose an interesting name, one that reminds you of your inner calm, purpose, and sense of adventure.

Here are some actual names. How about "New Horizons"? or "Clear Sailing"? Indian names are often very interesting and descriptive. "Flexible Arrow"? "Chief White Cloud"? How about "Instinctively on Target"? "Rolling Easy"? or "Mellow Tourist"? Some persons have used metaphors from nature such as "Flowerbed" and "Mountain High." Nature offers excellent self-images. Perhaps you'd like to be more concrete. Consider "Mr. or Ms. Prosperity," "Mr. Pleasure" or "Miss Fantastic Life," "Total Success," "Chief Executive in Charge of Me," even "Execupower, Inc."

Write the name that you have chosen for yourself in the margins of this book. If, after awhile, it doesn't sit perfectly with you, then by all means discard it and choose another. In any case, it's imperative that you once and for all decide who you really are, entirely on your own terms. Philosophers, psychologists, and theologians don't often agree, but they do agree on one thing: there is no absolute definition regarding the nature of man. So, do as all FEEs have done; take advantage of this power vacuum and define yourself on your own terms and in a way that will do you the maximum amount of good.

My personal definition has long been "Gentle Flowing Brook." I have derived a very deep and satisfying sense of self from this inner picture. I see my particular brook moving calmly along (inner calm) toward some fantastically beautiful glacier lake off in the distance somewhere (purpose). My brook also has serendipitous turns and surprises, and occasional white waters. This adds adventure and excitement to my life. I can see myself this way whenever I want to. If I should get nervous for one reason or another, I've learned to remind myself that I'm a gentle flowing brook and say to myself, "Hey Kushel, what's a brook like you got to be nervous about?" And I calm down, almost immediately. This method of FEEs really works.

FEE Jim Edwards believes that our universe has a constant hum. "This is a cosmic flow, and experiencing this cosmic flow is readily available for everyone to enjoy. All we need do as human beings is tune in to it." Jim is an electronics expert and likens human beings to radio receivers. "We really can readily tune in or tune out any sounds that we want. Many persons tune into static and noise. They miss listening to the beautiful sounds of the universe that are always being transmitted. All we need do is to tune in to the proper station and there it is. Jim's inner picture was "Cosmic Flow." He said he sometimes said to himself, "Go, go with the Cosmic Flow!" From all appearances, his inner picture worked very well for him.

The Choice Is Always Yours: Use Execupower

Situation: You've just been avoided deliberately by the regional boss at a meeting. You feel rejected.

Self-Defeating Thought
He hurt my feelings.

Fully Effective Thought
I chose thoughts which hurt my feelings. I don't like having hurt feelings; therefore, I'll choose more effective thoughts. It wasn't really me that he avoided, it was just his image of me. I can't be responsible for what he sees, thinks, and feels. In order to reject me, someone has to know me, has to really listen and care for me on my own terms. And if he were to do that, I couldn't possibly be rejected.

FEE Bob Rosenberg named his inner self, "One Man's Dream." His dream went as follows: "I see myself as this fantastic tall ship, well constructed, great sails, a sturdy rigging, a balanced compass. I'm manned with an excellent, experienced crew and we have a storeroom filled with provisions for an exciting journey. I see this ship underway on the high seas. I'm not at all fearful of the rolling sea because this ship is sturdy and sound, with a good rudder. Even in the tossing sea, I feel calm and purposeful. The ship is headed to an exotic, distant port. I'm going somewhere that's fantastic—Tahiti, or someplace like that."

Rosenberg returned to this inner self-picture numerous times: "Being a 'Tall Ship' is a source of courage. It helps me face adversity. Being a 'Tall Ship' makes me feel purposeful even in spite of what sometimes seems circuitous and empty in the circus of daily events." Developing a clear sense of individual purpose is very difficult for many persons. "Tell me what to do, and I'll do it. I need leadership," so many people say. But FEEs have their own goals that others often plug into.

The Choice Is Always Yours: Use Execupower

Situation: You've made a serious business error.

Self-Defeating Thought	Fully Effective Thought
I fouled up. I'm just no good.	I fouled up. I can take full responsibility for my mistake. My mistake is an error in behavior. But I am much more than behavior. I am the sum total of what I think.

When attempting to have a purposeful life, many persons tend to establish more material possessions, gains on the job, and fame as their chief goals. But the purposes of FEEs went beyond these important but often insufficient and sometimes impossible to attain goals. FEEs' goals often included the development of successful human relationships and the completion of certain projects—projects that are in harmony with their larger purposes.

FEE Phil Roberts: "I have as the major purpose of my life a strong desire to be a very loving person and friend. I genuinely enjoy my job, but it's the loving of my family and the loving of certain key friends that matters the most to me. Someday, this big job of mine may not be there.

"But I will always be there for my family and true friends. Whether they do the same for me or not is not really under my control. I realize that. I'm definitely the one in charge of whether I choose to love or not to love somebody. That's why my chief purpose—to be a loving human being—is so satisfying for me. It's fully under my own control."

FEE Max Vogel had as his major goal designing and building a summer home from blueprint to finished product. "This project, I must admit, has kept me out of lots of trouble at work. I'm totally preoccupied with it. You see, I have a tremendous amount of creative energy, and if that energy was not channelled properly, I could get into an awful lot of trouble here at the office. But my spare time project keeps me thinking. I work on it all the time, in my mind and then on weekends and vacations. My summer house project keeps me very excited and on the go.

"I always feel that I have something very important going on and I'm building it all with my own hands. There's not enough work with my hands on my job. Building, designing, crafting is something that is fully under my own control and that's important to me. Of course the planning takes a lot of the time and I figure that I might never get it completely built. I've been working on it piecemeal, bit by bit, for over four years now. But whether it finally gets completed or not isn't the major factor. It's the process, the working on it that counts the most for me. The end is never where it appears to be anyhow." Max's inner self-image? "Summer House," of course.

The Choice Is Always Yours: Use Execupower

Situation: You are aware that you lack needed computer literacy and fluency.

Self-Defeating Thought	Fully Effective Thought
Who you know is infinitely more important than what you know. I can get someone to know what I need to know.	Who I know is very important. But what I know is important too. I can learn anything that I set my mind to, if I take it at my own rate of speed.

FEE Mike Richman's passion was his garden. "I take my

gardening hobby more seriously than I take my work," said Richman. "If it wasn't for gardening, I think that I would have been wiped out long ago with a bad case of nerves. Worldwide strategic planning, these days, is not the perfect occupation for a sensitive person like me, but gardening is. I may not make my living in the garden, but I do make my life there."

The Choice Is Always Yours: Use Execupower

Situation: The big project that you headed up ends as a disaster.

Self-Defeating Thought	**Fully Effective Thought**
My project bombed. I've failed.	My project failed. But I'm not my project. I've a clear inner identity that can never fail.

FEEs all had something big going on inside of themselves that usually had little or nothing to do with earning a living. This special project consistently met three criteria: It was fully under their own control, not subject to outside interference; it gave the FEE a sense of larger purposes; and the time for completion of the project was entirely up to the FEE and no one else.

FEEs know that deadlines can kill. If there were rigid time constraints on their project, they managed to ease out of these deadlines at least psychologically by saying to themselves "If the deadline is not met I will consider the project successful anyway."

All too often, our professional practices meet with a great deal of interference by uninformed or uncaring others. Too often there are inane committees that sit in judgment of creative ideas. Too often these are bureaucratic boards to satisfy, or difficult customers with uncultivated tastes that have the say over one's accomplishments. But with the FEE's special project, there is no such interference of any consequence that can keep the FEE from achieving his goals.

The Choice Is Always Yours: Use Execupower

Situation: You are shocked to find that your reputation has been badly tainted by exaggerated, unkind professional gossip.

Self-Defeating Thought	**Fully Effective Thought**
I'm really destroyed. I've been ruined. It's so unfair. I'm furious.	I'll do what I can to straighten this mess out. But I'm not my reputation. Who I am is clear to me. I am not responsible for what others choose to think about me. I can only influence others opinion of me, but I can never fully control what others choose to think of me. I control only what I think about myself. I know who I really am.

The FEE's project, be it gardening, building, writing, painting, designing, creating, or playing has only one opinion about it that really matters. That is the opinion of the "Chief Project Director," the FEE himself.

FEE Neil Evans: "I take my golf game more seriously than my work. I realize that I'm never going to make a living as a golf pro, so when I play, I compete only against myself. There's always some new stroke that I'm trying to perfect or a new angle about the game that completely preoccupies me. If I were to ever take the winning of tournaments with total seriousness, the game wouldn't have the same value for me. Believe me, there's enough competition at work. I don't need more of that with my greatest pleasure. But I do want you to know, I've won more than my share of tournaments and it's probably because I don't have to win that I do win."

Once you settle on an exciting inner identity, a large variety of Fully Effective Thoughts will automatically rise up out of your subconscious. In the best sense of the word, you will have "reprogrammed" your subconscious to produce an ongoing scenario that encompasses your entire life. As you act in harmony with your inner vision of self, easy living becomes yours in spite of any external circumstances that would upset the "average" person.

FEEs, because of their free-flowing self-pictures, tend to have very positive affects on those who work around them. "Many people tell me I'm a good influence on them," said FEE Ted Rogers. "They find me supportive and inspiring, so they say. I believe them."

FEE Mike Richman, because of his inner identity, tended to be in touch with larger forces. "Recently up in Maine I took a siesta on the rocks at Acadia overlooking the Atlantic. I felt part and parcel of the ocean. I felt a oneness with the easy gliding of the sea gulls on gentle currents of wind. Everything seemed to blend together into some unified force and I was part of it." As Richman spoke I could sense the enormity of this experience for him. Richman said, "This oneness is ever present. All I need do now is tune into it whenever I want to. I continuously take trips to my place on the rocks at Acadia, even during business meetings that used to kill me slowly with boredom and tension." Next time that you are faced with a boring meeting, why not tune into something more beautiful and interesting than that which is going on in the room. The method works to escape the nagging of a spouse, a noisy child, or the dominance of your boss. Tuning in to a more pleasurable inner existence is always a live option.

The Choice Is Always Yours: Use Execupower

Situation: You've just been given a warm and sincere compliment by someone.

Self-Defeating Thought	**Fully Effective Thought**
How embarrassing. I wonder what they're after? I'd better compliment them somehow in return too.	I appreciate that. Thanks. Feels good.

The following Hidden Identity Rehearsals require that you create fully effective thoughts constructed around a soundly conceived hidden identity. How does a hidden identity help one to deal more effectively with each of the following situations? Remember, whenever necessary, choose your hidden identity instead of relying solely on job title or roles that you play.

- Your records are under intensive audit by your company. They have not been up to company standards and you know it.
- Your professional reputation has been tarnished by unfavorable gossip.
- Too much extra work is being heaped upon you. You can't keep up with it all, and yet even more work is tossed your way.
- One of your superiors tends to intimidate you with his overbearing manner.
- You are at a social gathering with many important people. You feel inferior to most of them.
- You've been called to be interviewed regarding an important special assignment that you really want. However, you don't feel up to the interview just now.

Combine your newly conceived hidden identity with what you have learned in the previous chapter about the Reality Practice. Use the Execupower Principle to create Fully Effective Thoughts to overcome each of the aforementioned situations. The Execupower guidesheet in Chapter 4 offers a complete approach with internal and external attacks. All of this is an important part of the Execupower System. The Execupower Principle, plus the fully effective thoughts inherent in both the Reality and Hidden Identity Practice are an excellent beginning. Still to come are four other equally powerful practices and derivative thoughts. Below is a chart that contrasts how FEEs and SDEs might handle the obvious trauma of being summarily fired.

Type I, The Total Victim, has not mastered either the Reality Practice or the Hidden Identity Practice. Obviously, he's in very big trouble when his job carpet is pulled out from under him.

Type II, The Hard-Driver, because he has a good sense about the facts of life and knew, perhaps, that his job wasn't as secure as

Situation: You are fired from your job suddenly, through no fault of your own.

	Has Not Mastered The Reality Practice "Be Reasonable"	Has Mastered The Reality Practice "Be Realistic, Not Merely Reasonable"
Has not mastered The Hidden Identity Practice. "I'm my job, title, family role, etc."	Self-Defeating Executive Type I *The Total Victim* "I'm shocked; at a complete loss. What will I do? What will I do?"	Self-Defeating Executive Type II *The Hard-Driver* "I knew this could happen, but I'm crushed. My job meant everything to me."
Has mastered The Hidden Identity Practice. "I'm my . . . *(hidden identity)."*	Self-Defeating Executive Type III *The Dreamer* "I'm dumb. I can't believe it. At least, there are other aspects of life that I've still got going for me."	The Fully Effective Executive Type IV *The Healthy Skeptic* "I knew this was always a possibility. Fortunately, I've got my back-up identity on reserve. When the going gets tough, that's when I really get going."

it appeared on the surface (the Reality Practice) is not in the same degree of trouble. But he is in some trouble nonetheless, because he had no Hidden Identity to back him up now that his job has been terminated. He'll now have a tendency to be much too intense in his job search, and probably lose out more often than he needs to.

Type III, The Dreamer, has a clear inner identity, but a poor sense of the Reality Practice. Losing his job is very surprising since he was so naive. But with a sound hidden identity, he'll not be in trauma, and will bounce back with resiliency and conduct a successful job search.

And of course, Type IV, The Healthy Skeptic, is probably an FEE. He's mastered both the Reality Practice and The Hidden Identity Practice, and more than likely, the four other remaining practices that we've yet to discuss. He'll face the reality of the job loss, remind himself of his hidden identity, continue his exciting life, and conduct a successful job search handling everything in optimal fashion.

The point here is that it is important to use the one principle and all six practices if you are to be fully effective. One principle in isolation might be helpful, but it doesn't have the exceptional payoff that mastering the complete system will have for you.

If Type III, the Dreamer, on the chart eventually masters the Reality Practice, he might be on his way to Fully Effective status, while Type I, Total Victim, characterizes many seriously depressed and neurotic persons. They have yet to master *any* practices mentioned here.

The next practice of FEEs is the Eustress Practice. As you know, stress often kills and can certainly keep you from enjoying your life. However, FEEs do not avoid stress. They are, in fact, *stress-seekers*. Eustress is a very special kind of productive stress. Once you learn how to attain eustress, rather than distress, you'll never be the same.

Turn now to the Eustress Practice of FEEs.

7

THE EUSTRESS PRACTICE

Fully Effective Thought #3:
"Seek Eustress, Not Distress."

Even though most FEEs have pressure cooker jobs, their lives are relatively stress-free. Moreover, they do not run from stress, but rather are avid stress-seekers. How do they do this? Consistent with Execupower Theory, they simply choose effective, stress-reducing thoughts as needed. In other words, FEEs just don't experience the same kinds of stress that less effective persons do.

They do experience something called "eustress" (coined by Dr. Hans Selye, the noted Canadian authority on stress). Eustress is the opposite of distress. *"Eu"* in Greek means good, hence eustress means "good stress." As you would expect, the FEEs' eustress comes about by the special eustressful thoughts that they choose. They consistently take it upon themselves to look at any situation, no matter how stressful it might seem to another person, in such a way that it causes them no anxiety whatsoever. Whenever necessary, they pause, then choose eustressful, not distressful, thoughts. You can always choose thoughts that produce feelings of calm, or if the situation warrants, a quantity of creative, eustressful tension. Not all tension is useless. A certain creative anxiety can prompt you to get that difficult job done, make that hard-to-make telephone call, or stand up to that overbearing authority figure that's been troubling you.

However, in America today, there is rampant indulgence in tranquilizing drugs, alcohol, and other substances designed to help nervous persons to escape from excessive stress and tension, both at home and at work. Also, millions of persons overeat in their efforts to relieve tension. More recently, young women especially, are resorting to bulemic and anorexic behavior, trying to look better so that they can feel better about themselves. All of these drastic measures are, of course, clearly self-defeating.

FEEs merely choose eustressful thoughts in order to sustain healthy levels of inner calm. They never need to resort to drug abuse so that they might enjoy life, since there is no reason for them to escape from something as satisfying as eustress.

There are huge numbers of frantic success-seekers who are suffering the consequences of too much stress: heart disease, hypertension, and other physical ailments. FEEs, however, achieve their success without such damage. They realize that most distress results primarily from unnecessary fears. FEE Bob Rosenberg: "Most of the fears that people experience are rarely justified by the facts." President Franklin D. Roosevelt: "The only thing we have to fear is fear itself."

FEEs eliminate all nonproductive fear simply by choosing effective thoughts about fear. All of the strong emotions such as anger, jealousy, bitterness, anxiety, and guilt are derived primarily from unjustified fears—fears that are the product of self-defeating rather than fully effective thinking.

If you suddenly heard a loud bang, you'd likely jump. The

noise, frightening you, would cause you to put your entire nervous system on alert. Your glands would produce a quick shot of adrenalin that would spread throughout your entire body. Fear would stimulate, almost instantly, the well-known "fight or flight" response. The "fight or flight" alert results in anger. In fact, if you found out that an unruly child had dropped a firecracker under your child as a practical joke, you might be quite angry for awhile. Again, your anger stemmed directly from fear. FEE Ted Barton: "When I see someone who is very angry, I realize that I am looking at someone who is very frightened. I ask, what is he so frightened about? And I do the same thing for myself. When I get very angry, I pause, then I say to myself, 'Ted Barton, what are you so afraid of?' At first it's difficult for me to get in the frame of mind to examine my fears, especially when I'm angry. But when I do, I usually find that what I'm afraid of has no rational basis. So then the fear goes away, and with that, so does all the anger."

Staying on a constant fear alert in a jungle or a battle zone makes some sense. But it is unwarranted in most everyday life situations and wreaks havoc with your nervous system. Certainly a sudden loud bang deserves to shock you into a position of alert. But if it was only a child's toy balloon that had popped, you certainly wouldn't run. And as your unwarranted fear disappeared (because of your new thoughts), the temporary anger would soon leave also.

Unfortunately, far too many persons spend whole lives alerted by unjustified and unwarranted fears. Most fears are produced by self-defeating thoughts. By constantly living in fear, tension becomes a veritable lifestyle and naturally puts a severe strain on our health. While Self-Defeating Executives seldom give their nervous systems rest, FEEs always take numerous mini-vacations each and every day.

FEE Phil Roberts: "I tithe. Every day I give at least 10 percent of my time to terrific inner pleasure and rest. Most days, in fact, I cheat. I take even more than my 10 percent quota. I'm for easy livin'." Thoreau said "most persons live lives of quiet desperation." While that may be true, in my work with FEEs, I found a group of persons who were living lives of quiet exhilaration and tremendous inner calm, rather than lives of desperation and nervousness.

Each of us was born small and highly dependent. But also, as infants we had an innate ability to be cared for, to be listened to, to be loved and attended to. For most of us, little by little, bit by bit, life chipped away at this originally positive sense of basic self-esteem, perhaps by simply being left crying a bit too long for milk, or in a wet diaper. As an infant, many of us erroneously concluded we'd been abandoned. Still helpless and totally dependent, most infants have a terrible fear of being abandoned. Most of the time such fears are not justified. Parents are not abandoning their children simply because they aren't around at that exact moment the infant desired them. But the infant doesn't reason that out, and is often left with a growing sense of fear— fear that he is not all that lovable.

As adults, we still feel as if we are about to be abandoned, and we often operate with this irrational fear lurking insidiously in our subconscious. Many people manifest a sense of generalized anxiety and tension, but can find nothing in particular to put their finger on. But all FEEs have figured out for themselves that their basic fear of being abandoned is totally irrational. As adults, they have decided for themselves to feel just as lovable and as able to be listened to and cared for by others as they were when they were just born. FEEs, with their original level of high self-esteem very much intact, don't experience the generalized nervousness and anxiety that results from an irrational fear of being abandoned.

Without irrational fear as their base, FEEs easily avoid the consequences of excessive anger, anxiety, and nervousness.

The Choice Is Always Yours: Use Execupower

Situation: You find yourself falling in love with someone. You believe such involvement is not in your best interest.

Self-Defeating Thought	Fully Effective Thought
She (he) really turns me on. I can't help myself.	My thoughts about her (him) are turning me on. I can and will choose more effective thoughts that will better serve my best professional and personal interests. I can choose thoughts about this person that will turn me off. For example, I can exaggerate in my mind any flaws this person has. After all, I can think anything I want to think.

Since all of the negative, totally nonproductive emotions stem only from irrational fear, FEEs easily control these untoward emotions. Excessive anxiety, jealousy, depression, and guilt are all learned modes of emotional expression and have as their root cause, irrational fear. And that which has been learned can just as easily be unlearned.

When a child is taken to the playground for the first time and hears other playing children yelling and screaming, he naturally becomes frightened. The child grasps his mother's hand in a cold sweat and his mother comfortingly explains, "Bobby, it's all right. Yelling and screaming is just part of playing. You need not fear," Bobby learns that loud yells and screams need not always produce fear. Fears are often learned products of perception.

Gradually we develop an expansive emotional vocabulary that includes concepts like jealousy, worry, ecstasy, joy, guilt, and depression. All these emotions are derived from fear. As an FEE chooses thoughts that extinguish unnecessary fears, then each of these unwanted negative emotions can be readily controlled.

Since 97% of all that we fear probably never takes place, those FEEs who have only rational, reality-based fears experience only about 3% of the stress that less effective persons experience. About 97% of the time FEEs remain stress-free, while other persons suffer.

On those few occasions that fear is actually justified, FEEs experience fear also. They wisely fear passing other cars on narrow roads at high speeds. They fear walking a tightrope, if they have no experience on the high wire. They wisely fear violence, bombs, maniacs, drugs they know little about, and large, out of control mobs.

The Choice Is Always Yours: Use Execupower

Situation: You are seemingly uncontrollably jealous about another person's activities.

Self-Defeating Thought
This jealousy is justified. I can't do much about it.

Fully Effective Thought
My excessive jealousy comes from fear. My fear results from an absence of sufficient self-esteem. I will choose thoughts to raise my self-esteem, reduce my fear, and control my jealousy.

Drs. Friedman and Rosenman, distinguished cardiologists, researched the probable causes of heart disease. Previous to their study it was commonly believed that heart disease was caused primarily by a combination of high cholesterol, hypertension, being overweight, excessive smoking, and insufficient exercise. However, Friedman and Rosenman's study concluded that an individual's particular pattern of behavior was a far more important factor leading to heart disease than any of the foregoing.

Those most prone to heart disease exhibited a pattern of behavior that Friedman and Rosenman labeled *Type A Behavior.* Type A persons continuously feel a tremendous, sense of pressure, both professionally and personally. Type A's see themselves as involved in a chronic struggle with life. As hard-drivers, Type A's often manifest also the characteristics ascribed to the "workaholic." They seem to feel as if there is always some serious deadline that if not met spells certain disaster. They live and function under heavy stress.

Type B personalities, on the other hand, are easygoing and relaxed. FEEs have a great deal in common with Friedman and Rosenman's Type B's. FEEs, for example, have a way of looking at so-called deadlines in such a way that leaves little room for stress.

FEE Larry Burns: "While I always try to meet my goals in the time that I've set, if I see that meeting a particular deadline is going to put a tremendous strain on me, I simply figure out how I'll handle the situation even if my deadline isn't met. Inevitably, I figure a way out and as soon as I do, the stress of the deadline automatically disappears. Then I still do what I have to in order to meet my original deadline, but I now know in advance that it won't be the end of the world if I don't meet it."

FEEs always establish realistic rather than reasonable time-tables. Moreover, they are not obsessed with achieving external success, although they are obsessed with enjoying their lives. FEE Mike Richman: "It's strange. When I tried so hard, years ago, I never seemed to be able to make it. Now that I take it much easier, so many more things seem to go my way—and all with practically no internal strain whatsoever."

The Choice Is Always Yours: Use Execupower

Situation: Your Federal Income Tax returns are called for a special audit by the Internal Revenue Service.

Self-Defeating Thought
I'm in big trouble now. My number is up. I'll be destroyed. Why does Uncle Sam have to pick on me?

Fully Effective Thought
My returns reflect appropriate tax shelter devices. If all is not correct, I'll make the appropriate adjustments. I know that there is no such thing as 'absolute justice.' Anyone can be selected for an audit. Whatever happens, I'll be able to handle it; I know that for sure.

FEEs always maintain the proper balance between work and play. Type A's, like the self-defeating persons of my study, took work much too seriously and took play much too lightly. FEE Bob Rosenberg: "I take my work as a game and I take 'enjoying life' as something extremely important and essential." But Type A's take work all too seriously.

Type A's are often out of breath, rushing to express two opposing thoughts at the same time. Type A's walk too fast, eat too much in a hurry, and even move very quickly (often in circles) seated at their desks. They tend to rush their conversations. Sadly, Type A's are very impatient, and usually become extremely irritated when waiting in line at banks, supermarkets, and restaurants. They also become overanxious when watching others do things that they believe they themselves can do faster or better. Type A's also resent the necessary, but slow moving, activities such as writing checks and balancing checkbooks. Moreover, Type A's rarely listen intently to others. They are too preoccupied spinning their own wheels nervously on a trip to nowhere in particular.

The Choice Is Always Yours: Use Execupower

Situation: Work continues to pile up on your desk. There are many phone calls and other interruptions. You feel overloaded and stressed.

Self-Defeating Thought	**Fully Effective Thought**
I can do anything that comes my way. I may go crazy, but I'll get it done.	I am going to edit and organize my day. I'll give each pressure a number, put it in line, and treat it according to priority. I'll deal important, but one thing at a time. For me, it's always quality over quantity. I can't be all things to all people.

Instead of listening carefully to others, Type A's are preoccupied with worry about what they have to do next. Type A's often compulsively brag, having to tell others about their latest achievements and accomplishments. They are competitors to a fault, competing out of need, not preference. They have the need to always come out on top in everything, even in recreational sports. Type A's fret and fume if they lose a friendly tennis match. Obviously, Type A's are the perfect candidates for an Execupower Program. If you know any, or are one yourself, get Execupower going immediately.

FEEs are very much like Type B's and not at all like the heart attack prone Type A's. However, the FEEs' attitudes may not always appear on the surface. In fact, those who don't really know an FEE beyond his veneer can easily mistake him for a Type A. FEEs are not always as they appear to be. FEEs may move rapidly on specific occasions, but always do so only when moving fast makes particular sense, as it sometimes does in certain situations. They sometimes even feign worry, if such pretending is productive in a particular situation. However, FEEs seldom really worry because worry serves no useful function. Instead of worrying, FEEs generally concentrate directly on the job at hand, rather than worry about something that isn't facing them at the moment. They replace worry with due concern. By pausing and readily choosing eustressful thoughts, instead of stressful thoughts, they prevent nervousness and heart disease.

The Choice Is Always Yours: Use Execupower

Situation: You're left waiting in line and become late for another obligation simply because the clerks take an extended coffee break.

Self-Defeating Thought	**Fully Effective Thought**
I'm furious. I'm becoming a nervous wreck just seething and waiting for those clerks to finish their coffee. Some nerve.	This isn't right. I'll go over there and speak nicely but firmly to them. If I'm late for my next appointment, I'll be able to deal with that effectively. I vow that I will have another excellent day in spite of this circumstance.

An extremely useful technique that FEEs regularly use to help themselves slow down is "Calming Self-Talk." I've provided such a script for you. All you need to do is tape record your voice, repeating the following script slowly into the tape recorder. Then play it back to yourself two or three times daily, or as often as needed. If you let fully effective "slow-down" thoughts penetrate, eventually, choosing such thoughts will become a matter of habit.

Instructions: Read the following relaxation script very slowly into a tape recorder. Pauses as indicated are for about six seconds each. Find a comfortable place and play this recording as needed.

The Calming Self-Talk Script

"Place yourself in a comfortable place. (pause) Loosen your collar, put your feet on the floor, and place your hands comfortably on your lap. (pause) Now lean back and take a nice, long, easy, deep breath. Inhale slowly, hold, then exhale slowly. (pause) Remember, inhale slowly. (pause) Then exhale. (pause) Good.

"Now shut your eyes tight. (pause) Tight, tighter. (pause) All right, now let your eyelids relax completely. (pause) Let all of the tiny muscles in your eyelids ease up. Let out all tension now. (pause) Let all tension completely out of your eyelids. (pause That's right. Now make the muscles of your forehead tight. (pause) Make them even tighter. (pause) Tighter still. (pause) All right, now let your forehead relax completely. Take a slow, deep breath. (pause) Hold. Then exhale. (pause) Make the back of your neck tense. (pause) Now let all of the muscles in the back of your neck relax completely. (pause) Relax all of the muscles at the back of your neck and let all of the tension ease out of the back of your neck right now. (pause) Take another nice, deep breath; hold, then exhale slowly. (pause) Good.

"Now relax. (pause) Now experience your jaw; tense your upper and lower jaw and then separate your jaws ever so slightly. (pause) Tighten your lower and upper jaws. (pause) Tighter. (pause) Tighter still. (pause) Good. Now relax your jaws. (pause) Let your upper and lower jaw separate ever so slightly and now

let out all of the tension of your jaws. (pause) That's right, all of the tension out of your jaws. (pause) Again, take a nice slow deep breath, hold, then relax. (pause) Good. You're now getting very, very much at ease. (pause) Now experience and tense your right shoulder. (pause) That's right. (pause) Tense your shoulder, then let it relax. (pause) Let your right shoulder relax completely. (pause) That's very good. Now tense your left shoulder. (pause) Make it tense. (pause) Good. Now let all of the tension out of your right shoulder. (pause) And now your left shoulder. (pause) Make your left shoulder tight, tight. (pause) Tighter still. (pause) Let all of the tension out of your left shoulder. (pause) Now let both of your arms get very tense. (pause) Good. Now let them get very relaxed, heavy and tired. (pause) Very, very tired. (pause) Your arms are now very, very heavy. Very, very tired. (pause) Let all the tension out of your arms. All of the tension out of both of your arms right now. (pause) That's very good. (pause)

"And now experience your spinal column. Just be aware of your spinal column. Just notice it. (pause) It's been there for a long time. Now just let your spinal column relax completely. (pause) Let all of the tension, all of the tense knots and muscles around your spinal column ease up so that your entire spine is very much at ease. (pause) Now make your buttocks very tense. (pause) Make your buttocks very tense. (pause) Now let your buttocks relax ever so comfortably. Feel very, very much at ease. (pause) Take a deep, easy breath. Inhale slowly. Hold. Then, exhale slowly. (pause) That's right. Very good. (pause) And now make your left leg tense. (pause) Make your left leg very tense. Make your entire left leg rigidly tight. (pause) Make it tighter. Tighter still. (pause) And now let your left leg relax completely. (pause) Let your left leg relax completely. (pause) Breathe in. Hold. Breathe out slowly. (pause) Completely relax now. (pause) And now, experience your right leg. Make your right leg very tight, very tense. (pause) Tight and tense. That's right. (pause) Now let your right leg relax completely. (pause) Again, take a nice deep breath. Airs of relaxation in, hold, then tension out. (pause) At this point, you're feeling very, very comfortable. You

are now very much at ease. (pause) Your legs are very heavy and
tired. Your buttocks are very heavy and tired. Your back is very
relaxed and heavy and tired, and your shoulders are very heavy
and tired. Your arms and your neck, your forehead, your eyes,
your face, your throat are all very heavy, tired, and completely
relaxed. (pause) Totally at ease. (pause)

"You're feeling very much at ease now. You feel very calm.
Very, very comfortable. (pause) You haven't been this calm and
comfortable in a long, long time. (pause) Now balance your inner
compass and let plenty of relaxation into your mind and let all
tension ease out. (pause at this point for about 10 to 15 seconds)
In a moment, I will count to three, and with each number you
will feel more and more refreshed and relaxed. (pause) When I
say 'three' you will open your eyes slowly and you will feel
completely relaxed and refreshed as if you have just finished
many hours of very peaceful sleep. (pause) One. (pause) You're
feeling very refreshed. (pause) Two. You're feeling excellent and
restful now. (pause) And three. You are wide awake now and are
feeling completely relaxed and refreshed."

Use this *Calming Self-Talk Method* as often as necessary to
relax yourself. After using it consistently, you will eventually find
many calming thoughts coming to mind as a matter of course.
Calming Self-Talk certainly beats taking drugs and alcohol as a
relief from stress. Calming Self-Talk is, in a sense, a meditative
experience. Again, in accordance with Execupower Theory, Theory E, you create your own feelings by choosing effective
thoughts. Why not choose effective eustressful thoughts instead of
self-defeating stress-producing thoughts?

Use the Calming Self-Talk script as an adjunct to the *ABC's of*
Choosing discussed previously. You can use this script in combination with the *Aggravation Technique.* Simply make yourself
excessively nervous by choosing nerve-wracking thoughts. Then
quickly take charge and talk yourself (through the calming self-
talk method) into feeling calm. Then you can also use Calming
Self-Talk in conjunction with B, the Branding Tactic. During the
part of the Branding Tactic where you say "green" to yourself for

the third time, bringing you into direct access to your subconscious mind, simply repeat the Calming Self-Talk Script verbatim, playing the tape. Then add at the end the statement, "I will feel very, very calm all day." With this entire series of calming thoughts branded deeply into your subconscious, you will have completely reprogrammed yourself to experience eustress instead of distress.

If still more help is needed, of course, C, the Closure Process, can be used to complete any unfinished business that is haunting you and interrupting your sense of inner calm. Closure is especially important for effectively dealing with major stress-producing issues such as the death of a loved one, loss of a job, divorce, and other serious unresolved issues.

As you may recall, the Closure Process requires that you move expediently through four stages: shock, wheeling and dealing, anger, and disappointment, to eventual closure. Choosing thoughts that expedite this movement through the various stages is essential. Of course, even FEEs sometimes require the assistance of a well-trained psychotherapist to assist them to closure of deep-seated, painful unfinished business. After closure, Calming Self-Talk becomes doubly effective.

In addition to choosing Calming thoughts, FEEs also intelligently use dieting and exercise to reduce stress. When overweight, there is, of course, excessive strain on one's body, creating stress. Many dieters, unfortunately gain back all the weight that they've lost, especially those dieters who resort to the fad, crash diets, once the dieting period is over. But FEEs always keep their weight under control, not by crash dieting, but rather by dieting as a way of life. FEEs have often retrained themselves to eat properly balanced, nutritious meals and they stick fastidiously to whatever diet they select, simply by choosing those particular thoughts that promote sound eating habits. Jack Evans, a well-built, healthy FEE said, "All diets work if only you stay on them."

"Exercising is my favorite stress reducer," said FEE and jogger Loretta Reese, "I love to exercise. Every morning, rain or shine, I go for my twenty-minute run. I don't try to break any records; I run just for a specified amount of time, not for distance, and definitely not to compete or show off to anyone else. And I don't jog for muscles either. I jog for the pleasure I get from it and for the release from stress that it affords me.

Jogging gives me the chance to be alone with myself for a little while and I feel as if I am doing something really good for myself. Whether I am or not doesn't really matter; it's how I feel that matters. I find that jogging is even more help to me mentally than it is physically. And after my jog each morning, I feel ready to take on the world. It makes me feel ahead of the game."

Some joggers injure themselves by running too hard. Compulsive joggers sometimes injure their ankles and legs, and develop lower back pains. But since FEEs avoid compulsive behavior in most everything (except in having a terrific life), they rarely run to beat records, unless the record they're trying to beat is their own.

You will be able to discern which of the following thoughts regarding stress are fully effective and which are self-defeating. Place a check mark next to each fully effective thought and verify your answers at the end.

_____ 1. I'm overburdened. But you can always count on me. I'm good old reliable.

_____ 2. You can sometimes count on me—but not always. Let me decide if I really want to take on this additional assignment that you've heaped on my desk.

_____ 3. I'll take charge of my nervousness. I can choose any thought that I want, any time and place that I want to. It's my one inalienable right as a human being.

_____ 4. I can't help myself. Nervous thoughts just pop into my head. I don't choose them.

_____ 5. I have a choice as to whether I'll feel stressed or not. That person only has the illusion that he's my boss. I'm the real chief executive in charge of myself. He's merely playing the role of being my boss.

_____ 6. I'd better get moving. That's the boss's order from above.

_____ 7. I'm worried. I'm sure they're after me.

_____ 8. I have due concern, not worry. There's a big difference. I can handle anything that comes up.

The following thoughts were Fully Effective: numbers 2, 3, 5, and 8. The others were obviously self-defeating.

Now for some Eustress rehearsals. What effective thoughts derived from the Eustress Practice can help in the following situations?

1. You are faced with an urgent deadline. (Imagine an actual deadline that you may have faced at home or at work.) What fully effective thoughts can reduce probable tension in a situation such as this?

_____

_____

_____

2. Your teenaged son has just gotten his driver's license and is out on the road, well past midnight. There have been numerous serious car accidents at this late hour and you are extremely worried for his safety. How can you turn your natural distress into eustress in this particular situation? What fully effective thoughts might help? What techniques can you employ to remain calm?

_____

_____

_____

3. You are concerned about your professional reputation. You've just learned that certain jealous colleagues have besmirched your reputation by spreading unjustified, ugly rumors and gossip about the quality of your work. The injustice of all this really upsets you. Unfortunately, your boss is the type that is likely to believe these rumors without checking further. (1) How can the Eustress Practice assist you? (2) What specific thoughts can you choose to ease the natural tension resulting from this unpleasant circumstance?

Answers:

(1) _____

_____

(2) _____

_____

8

THE INFLUENCE PRACTICE

Fully Effective Thought #4: "Influence Others, Don't Try to Control Them."

FEEs experience a great deal of external, as well as internal, success. That is, they have big jobs, earn excellent salaries, and readily enjoy many material aspects of life. They attain their material success because they have mastered the practice of influencing others.

In order to move ahead in the corporate world, FEEs excel at team building, playing, and leading. The one fully effective thought that produces so much job success for them is "Influence others, don't try to control them."

There is a subtle, but extremely important distinction that must be made between influence and control. FEE Loretta Reese: "One of my salesmen was consistently late for meetings. I called him in. But instead of reprimanding him, I explained that he might be doing himself and the company a disservice. I don't feel that I wanted to totally control him, but I certainly had enough clout to influence him to be on time. All I had to do was point out the facts of the situation to him and let him figure out the rest for himself."

FEEs give their staff, family, and friends sufficient rope to manage their own lives—to make their own mistakes or to create their own successes. All FEEs enjoy a surplus of personal power since they are always in command of the thoughts that they choose. However, they rather quickly admit that they are never in charge of the thoughts that another person, a family member, boss, peer, or subordinate chooses to think. FEE Mike Richman: "If a person is able to choose any thought he wants to, no matter what the circumstance, then he is also in charge of what he feels and how he behaves." FEEs contend that there's no possible way at all, short of physical force, that one person can truly control another. All you can do about another's thought-choice is to influence what he chooses, not control what he chooses. The final choice is always up to the individual doing the choosing.

Suppose I wanted you to think well of me. I might strongly suggest that you choose thoughts along those lines. I can try to bribe you, plead my case, even promise to be your friend for life, if only you do as I suggest. I might act very friendly, even be a very decent, lovable human being, but ultimately the actual choice as to whether you'll do as I ask resides entirely with you. I might have some influence, but I definitely do not control you, or any other person for that matter.

To control you means that I can actually make you think, feel, and behave according to my desires. There's absolutely no chance of that, unless you were to completely abrogate your capacity to freely choose thoughts. Hence, all FEEs have learned to accept, to appreciate, to enjoy, and to master the art of influencing others.

Rodney Dangerfield, the comedian, is known for his "I get no respect," line. Obviously one can never demand respect and be sure to get it. One can only earn respect. One can demand homage or tribute and get it, but even though you can demand genuine respect all you want, you'll never be sure you'll get the real thing.

The Choice Is Always Yours: Use Execupower

Situation: Your boss disparages you in front of other members of the executive team.

Self-Defeating Thought	**Fully Effective Thought**
I'm devastated. I'm responsible for his negative talk. I could have controlled the way he acted. I'm disgusted with myself.	I can try to influence what he says about me to others, but I don't and can't control him. I'm not responsible for his thought-choices any more than he is responsible for mine. I can use some very clever influencing strategies, however, to prevent him from disparaging me like this ever again.

The FEE, through the exploitation of finely honed influencing skills, creates intrinsic motivation (as opposed to extrinsic motivation) in those who work with and for him. Less effective persons are often insufficiently sensitive to the important nuance between intrinsic motivation and extrinsic motivation. As you may know, with intrinsic motivation one has a proprietory interest in a given project or the success of a company or an idea. There is a sense of ownership and pride if you are involved in the development of something. But if something is foisted on you, extrinsic motivation, a forced motivation, ensues, e.g. "Do it because I said you should do it." Although both intrinsic and extrinsic motivation might get the job done, the intrinsically motivated worker emerges a self-starter, an initiator, a builder, who is proud and loyal to the cause under consideration.

The Choice Is Always Yours: Use Execupower

Situation: You want one of your staff to demonstrate more initiative and to be more loyal to the goals of the department.

Self-Defeating Thought	**Fully Effective Thought**
I'll get that son-of-a-gun to tow the mark. "Get going. We've got a big job to do. If you don't shape up, you'll soon be shipping out."	I'll influence him, not control him. There are a dozen ways of influencing at my disposal: setting a good example, positive reinforcement, appreciation, giving plenty of room for trial and error, etc. I'll let him become involved in the project at its inception.

FEE Ted Barton as head of an advertising agency sees himself as an influencer rather than a controller. Barton leads by example, and at the same time offers plenty of helpful guidance and assistance to his hard-working staff. He establishes a nurturant environment in which workers can take creative initiatives. Because he genuinely respects his staff, they reciprocate in kind. Barton realizes that although he cannot totally guarantee that he'll receive exactly what he deserves in return for all that he offers, such an attitude on his part can be very influential. Consequently, Barton does not *demand* respect; he simply makes it likely that he will receive respect by virtue of his influencing tactics, in this case, actually modeling the kind of behavior he expects in return.

FEE Ted Barton: "Intrinsic motivation lasts much longer than forced motivation. I can push my people, but if instead, I give people sufficient freedom to find their own way, they will be self-starters and contribute to this company for years to come. That's the kind of people that I like working for me. Self-starters, creative initiators, people with imagination that are loyal to me and the organization. I can't really insist on that and be sure to get it. I can only create the setting that makes it likely to happen."

Joanne came to me for counseling some time ago because she wanted "to have my husband appreciate me, to pay more attention to my needs. Yet everything I tried to make this happen didn't seem to work," she lamented. "I tried every single ploy that I could think of: compliments, sexual bribery, devotion; I even tried being the so-called ideal wife, whatever that is, but nothing whatsoever seemed to work."

When Joanne one day discovered that her husband was having an affair with her closest friend, she nearly had a complete nervous breakdown. "I tried everything that was humanly possible to make our marriage work. Where did I go wrong?" she asked. "I failed."

Joanne erroneously believed that she could actually have controlled the behavior of her wayward husband. Of course, that was an unrealistic expectation. One never *controls* another person, even if that other person is a spouse. Joanne's husband was totally responsible for his own actions. She, however, was completely responsible for herself, especially her feelings of failure.

As Joanne came to appreciate that she couldn't really control her husband, she also began to feel much less guilty and also began to free herself of her self-victimizing attitude. As Joanne fully appreciated that many events and people are definitely not under her own control, she took a greater interest in influencing more effectively. She gave up her foolish and impossible need to actually control her wayward husband.

FEE Neil Evans: "No matter how convincing or articulate a case I present, there is never a guarantee that my ideas will be accepted by someone else. So I present my case as eloquently and as articulately as possible. But the rest is up to the other guy."

FEEs capitalize on their high sounding job titles and their excellent positions within the corporate hierarchy since these are means of influencing people. But it is mainly their well-developed, often hard-earned, influencing skills that provided the biggest payoffs for them. These influencing skills were usually well instilled long before they became so externally successful, before they had such important jobs. In fact, it was these very influencing skills that got them these high level positions in the first place.

Long before they were a C.E.O., a President, or a Director, they were convincing others that their ideas were worthwhile and profitable, not only to the person they happened to be speaking with at that moment, but also to the organization that both of them worked for.

FEEs perceived each individual as being primarily motivated out of his or her own self-interest. Therefore, they go out of their way to ascertain what the self-interests of others are, then cater to these self-interests as much as possible, if they want to influence these persons. If they are successful in assisting others to achieve their goals or needs, they often become indispensable.

Successful influence requires creative motivation. There are numerous motivational techniques: carrots and M & M's (pats on the back), prods (warnings and penalties), and most importantly to FEEs, influential ideas. FEE Tom Bennett: "I'm known as a very influential person. But I'm not really all that powerful. It's just that I've got very persuasive ideas and use them." Influencing others requires intelligence, sensitivity, talents, and skills. FEEs successfully influence their bosses, colleagues, subordinates, friends, and family members with conventional communication and negotiation tactics.

For example, they carry themselves as if they are very successful in a given area long before they actually are. They make good use of powerful ideas, offer empathic listening to others, speak in regulated tones, and use concise writing to influence others effectively.

The Choice Is Always Yours: Use Execupower

Situation: You're required to meet with another division of your company at a conference scheduled for next week.

Self-Defeating Thought	**Fully Effective Thought**
First impressions aren't	First impressions are extremely

(Self-Defeating Thought)	*(Fully Effective Thought)* ·
particularly important.	powerful, much more powerful than they deserve to be. Therefore, I will do what I can to make the best first impression that I can. That's to my advantage. All I need do is figure out what kind of impression in this situation will be in my best interest and then go about making it.

Leonard and Natalie Zunin, a husband and wife research team, described in their book *Contact* how they systematically observed cocktail party behavior. They found that it generally takes *only four minutes* of contact between persons before a lasting impression is made. After only four minutes, most persons decide whether it appears to be worthwhile to spend any more time with someone they've just met.

Initial impressions apparently have so much impact that most of the time spent subsequent to the first impression is used to either validate or disprove that initial image. This, of course, is quite unfair to those persons who make first impressions that are not equal to what they really are. FEEs, however, use first impressions to great advantage.

Most of us prefer to believe that as wise and prudent individuals we will not put too much weight on our first impressions of others. But contrary to what we might like to believe, first impressions imprint deeply into our subconscious even when we try to keep that from happening. Even if we attempt to withhold our final judgment about a person that we've just met, that final judgment will still be based on proving whether or not our initial impression was valid or not. FEEs, knowing this, have as their policy to take the image that they project seriously. They know that success will be easier for them to achieve later on if they get off to a good early start.

FEE Vera Jennings: "I've found that after I've made a reasonably decent first impression, I can usually let my hair down, and then do things my way with a minimum of hassle. However, if I don't make a good first impression, then it takes me an enormous amount of doing to correct that bad start. Sometimes it takes forever to be forgiven for an early mistake, but mistakes made after I'm already well-thought-of are readily overlooked." FEE Jim Edwards: "If walking into a meeting with a big smile, a tie, and a three piece suit has payoff, and it does in my business, then I do it."

John Molloy, in *Dress for Success,* explained that according to his research, medium blue suits had maximum appeal to those in average socioeconomic brackets, whereas navy blue suits had maximum appeal to those in upper brackets. Since it is indeed possible that the shade of one's suit might make a difference, and since FEEs are pragmatic enough to want to have influence, they simply choose those thoughts that allow them to do so. Many other persons, less effective, and less professionally successful than FEEs might say, "The hell with all that image stuff. I dress the way I want. And if the world doesn't like it, fine. That's the world's loss, not mine." FEEs readily compromise themselves regarding principles that have no special validity for them. FEE Don Heath: "I have no interest in worrying about compromising my life, just because I compromise on the way I dress. I definitely realize that dress is quite superficial when you look at the larger picture. But I find it very easy to play the image game. It's because I appreciate the larger picture that I never waste my time insisting that I dress to suit my personality instead of dressing to influence others as needed."

The Choice Is Always Yours: Use Execupower

Situation: An order from "above": "As of next week, you will be required to wear a three-piece suit on the job."

Self-Defeating Thought	Fully Effective Thought
Not me. I don't go in for	What I wear isn't really me, but

(Self-Defeating Thought)
veneer. I'm into total
authenticity.

(Fully Effective Thought)
I know that the way I dress
influences others. I can easily
wear a vest and tie if I choose
to do so. And I choose to do
so.

FEEs do not have a need to influence others. They influence as a matter of preference. That is, their lives are in excellent order without having to influence others, because FEEs are highly autonomous individuals. They influence out of choice, not need. FEE Don Heath: "As Sophie Tucker said, 'I been rich and I been poor. And believe me, rich is better.' I don't have to hold this job or make big money, but I prefer doing well materially over not doing well materially. But deep down I know that I'd be quite satisfied selling hot dogs on the corner if push came to shove and I had to leave this 'important' job of mine."

As successful influencers, FEEs are excellent at reading body language and are sensitive as to what others might be thinking and feeling. But they are never so preoccupied with what others are thinking that others spoil their day. FEE Phil Roberts: "I might care what others are thinking, but I never feel responsible for what they're thinking. I can influence their thinking, but I'm not responsible for it. They are. I'm only totally responsible for what I think."

By using an artful blend of small talk, self-disclosure, productive listening, risk taking, and openness, FEEs become excellent administrators.

In order to influence effectively, it is essential that you know exactly how you are coming across to the person or persons you are attempting to influence. For example, if you wanted to sell a product, it would be invaluable for you to know what in particular motivates your prospective customer to buy. In so doing, it is essential that you be sensitive to the way that person probably perceives both you and the product you offer. FEEs who are in sales establish how they are being perceived by the person or persons that they desire to influence—positive, negative or neutral. They then do whatever is necessary to move forward from that point and make the sale.

FEEs are very much aware of how they are being perceived by others. Persons who are less effective too often try to influence in a vacuum, with little idea of how they actually come across to others. No wonder so many others are so much less successful than FEEs.

The following is a matrix that is commonly used in management training. It shows four different levels of interpersonal communication. The interaction between what one knows about himself and what is known by others about him results in four boxes reflecting four distinctive levels of interpersonal communication. Each of these four levels of interpersonal communication can be improved simply by choosing the following effective thoughts: Level I, "Enjoy just being, don't try too hard"; Level II, "Listen and care for others and you will get honest feedback in return"; Level III, "Use selective self-disclosure to build trust. Take a risk"; Level IV, "Remain open for surprising experiences."

A Management Training Tool

	Known to Self	Unknown to Self
Known to Others	LEVEL I *obvious material* "Nice day, isn't it?"	LEVEL II *feedback* "You don't look me in the eye when you speak."
Unknown to Others	LEVEL III *secrets* "I'm nervous."	LEVEL IV *metacommunication* "Something strange is happening, isn't it?"

At Level I, *Known to self and Known to others*   } This is
    1st person: "It's a beautiful day today, Miss   obvious
             Jones."   material
    2nd person: "Yes, it really is a gorgeous day."

At Level II, *Unknown to self, but Known to others*
    1st person: "You don't look me in the eye when   } getting
             you speak to me."   feedback
    2nd person: "Thanks for the feedback. I didn't
             know that I did that."

At Level III, *Known to self, but Unknown to others*
    1st person: "I'm very nervous."   sharing
    2nd person: "Interesting, I wouldn't have known it   secrets
             to look at you."

At Level IV, *Unknown to self, and Unknown to others*
    1st person: "Something strange is happening. I   meta-
             don't understand it."   communi-
    2nd person: "Yes, something strange is happening.   cation
             I don't understand it either."

The following Jo-Hari chart shows the fully effective thoughts that FEEs choose to make maximum use of at each of these levels of interpersonal communication.

	Known to Self	Unknown to Self
Known to Others	Level I: Interpersonal Communication—Enjoy just being. Don't try too hard.	Level II: Interpersonal Communication—Listen and care for others and you will get honest feedback in return.
Unknown to Others	Level III: Interpersonal Communication—Selective self-disclosure to build trust. Take a risk.	Level IV: Metacommunication (larger-than-life experiences)—Remain open for surprising experiences.

At Level I, communication is clear and nonsecretive. The information that is exchanged is known in advance by both parties. Often this is simply an exchange of the obvious. Level I communication is useful as reassurance. Small talk about the weather, ball scores, and routine gossip about the work as well as talk about such objective issues as budget cuts and office politics fit into this category.

Many executives have a difficult time with Level I small talk. They consider small talk a total waste of time. Others are simply afraid of it because it is usually ambiguous and indirect. One partially effective executive confided, "I can give a rousing speech to an audience of several hundred people with no problem whatsoever, but if you put me into an ambiguous situation, facing someone where all we need to do is to sit around and talk about nothing in particular, I'll get so damned uncomfortable that I could die." But FEEs include aimless small talk among their pleasures. In addition to simply enjoying it, they also find it invaluable as a pressure release. FEE Ed Hauser: "I love to waste time, sometimes, just talking about nothing in particular. Aimless small talk greases and lubricates the wheels of many business days."

FEE Philip Roberts: "While I prefer talking about really important matters, I realize that business isn't all there is to life. I find it extremely important to rest once in a while and slow down. I take little rests every day, right during working hours, for my mental health. Sometimes I tell crazy jokes that have no relevance whatsoever. And I must confess, I enjoy taking in the sexy good looks of some of the attractive women around here. Sometimes that's the only thing that keeps me going. Let's face it. Sex is everywhere. The way I figure it, I'm entitled to think anything I want, any time and place I want to, and sex is one of my most favorite subjects and pastimes. Hell, there's absolutely nothing wrong with thinking about sex at work. Of course there's a hell of a difference between thinking about it and acting on it. Look, I'm only passing this way once. If I don't take time out to enjoy myself, who will do it for me?"

FEE Bob Rosenberg, on long silences and blank stares that sometimes punctuate conversations: "I've learned to appreciate silence. Especially when I'm face to face with someone. Long silences don't tense me up like they used to when I was less secure. Now that I'm more comfortable with myself, I don't feel obliged to fill the air with the vapors of talk, just because I happen to be face to face with a tense person. There's absolutely nothing wrong with 'just being.' I don't always have to be 'on' or accomplishing something to feel worthwhile. Interestingly, since I've learned to enjoy long silences, I'm freer to talk only when I want to. And people listen to me more, too."

FEE Don Heath at one time resented the ritualistic social gatherings he was forced to attend because of his role as company president: "I basically hated those ritualistic company cocktail parties. But as president, I had to go to them. As a consequence, I taught myself to actually enjoy them. Why not? Since I had to attend, why not enjoy? I'm not much of a drinker, so at parties I generally carry around a glass filled with club soda and lemon. That way, no one bothers me to drink more than I want to. I fit right in, yet I do business my way. I wander around at those things and enjoy them. Half the time, I don't even pay attention to what people say to me at those events unless I'm really interested. Why should I?—I'm there symbolically, not as a person. They may need my body and the company gets it. But not necessarily my brain all the time. I make my job fun for myself. The job owns where I go and how I behave, but I'm the one always totally in charge of what I think." The fully effective thought for Level I situations is, "Sometimes just be; don't always try too hard."

The Choice Is Always Yours: Use Execupower

Situation: You're dying to tell all of your colleagues that you've just won the Award for Outstanding Professional Success, bestowed upon you by an outside professional group. Winning this award is very prestigious.

Self-Defeating Thought	**Fully Effective Thought**
Let me tell everyone. Why not? It really happened and I'm proud that I won it. I definitely want everyone to know, especially my colleagues. Some of them would give their right arm if only they could win it someday for themselves.	Colleagues may not be as enthusiastic about my receiving this outside honor as I am. Wiser not to say too much. In fact, it is wiser to keep my "glow" to myself for a couple days. If I still feel that I want to share, then I'll do it, but quite gently. People are sensitive.

Level II Interpersonal Communication, "what is known to others, but unknown to oneself," can only be communicated through feedback from those in the know. As others give you feedback, sharing their perceptions of how you come across to them, you then are in a better position to influence them. In order to get reliable feedback from others, it is important to leave yourself open to criticism occasionally. It is also important to permit yourself to be vulnerable, to really care at times about what others think and feel about you. And even leave yourself open to be hurt on occasion. If others do not sense that you really care for or value their honest opinions, especially those in positions subordinate to yours, they will often tell you only what they think you want to hear, rather than what you need to hear. After all, the Emperor who wore no clothes was never told he was naked. Openness to honest feedback would certainly have benefited him.

FEE James Geary: "At work it's often very difficult for me to find out how I'm genuinely coming across. There are so many people at the plant that have a vested interest in my opinion, so they're afraid to be as honest with me as I would like them to be. There's only one person there who has the guts to tell it to me like it is. That's because he knows I won't hold the truth against him. I need it, not just watered-down versions of the truth."

To counter the tendency of getting unauthentic feedback at work, many executives remove themselves periodically from company turf where they can get feedback from persons who are not threatened by their job title. The American Management Associations' "Executive Effectiveness" course is designed precisely for helping such executives get honest feedback away from home. A dozen or so key executives, all from different companies, retreat to a conference center and meet for a solid week at a time, 10 or 12 hours each day, doing little more than giving as much honest feedback to each other as truth-starved executives can handle. Their leveling with each other exemplifies the FEEs Fully Effective Thought for Level II situations: "Listen and care for others and you will get honest feedback in return."

Level III Interpersonal Communication requires that the executive risk honest self disclosure. At Level III you selectively share secrets with others about yourself: "I'm very nervous right now even though I may not appear that way," "I'm recently divorced and really upset over it," and "I'm terribly jealous of you." FEEs are only selectively open knowing what and when to share, depending on who is listening. FEEs are rarely indiscreet and foolish about sharing personal and professional secrets, but they do risk openness when it is appropriate.

FEE Ron Davis: "The difference between sharing personal secrets and professional secrets is considerable. I certainly don't want to be a complete mystery to those who work with me, but I don't want to be an open book either. However, since like usually begets like, I often risk being open. As I risk trusting others, it increases the potentiality for that person to also trust me, to be honest with me too. While being discreetly honest helps keep me informed about what's going on around the shop, at home with Betty, my wife, I can be totally honest. We love each other very much; there's a commitment. But at work it's different. It's a luxury not to have to have your guard up. Common sense tells me to be guarded at work." FEEs once again distinguish time, place, and circumstance and are only totally authentic when it makes good sense.

The Choice Is Always Yours: Use Execupower

Situation: A hard-working employee must be fired because of budget cuts.

Self-Defeating Thought	Fully Effective Thought
I have to fire John, so I'll be strong and tough and stay above his feelings. It hurts too much. "John, you're fired!"	I have to fire John, but I can still be sensitive and caring. I'll help him as much as I possibly can to find another job, perhaps even a better one. I'll share with him the hurt that I feel in having to let him go.

FEE Kevin Blake: "I think of myself as a very honest person. But if someone asks me the size of my bank account or wants to know the details of my sex life, I'll be damned if I'm going to be totally honest with him. Honesty always depends on the situation. If the risk makes sense, I'll share." The fully effective thoughts at Level III: "Be selective in your self-disclosure. Build trust. Take risks."

The Choice Is Always Yours: Use Execupower

Situation: You lack the know-how for a particular assignment.

Self-Defeating Thought	Fully Effective Thought
I'll look stupid if I ask for help. Let me figure it out myself.	It's only human not to know everything. It's important to get the necessary knowledge to do this job, and asking for help isn't always perceived as a sign of weakness or incompetence.

Level IV Interpersonal Communication is where that which is unknown to oneself dovetails with that which is unknown to others. Any communication at this level is metacommunication. Very mysterious. It is true that there are events, feelings, and things that we know little about, things that can't really be measured. Some feelings are communicated in ways that defy ordinary logic. Metacommunication often takes place in a non-verbal, seemingly magical way.

Since FEEs have a great deal of inner peace, they tend to be open to various larger-than-life, Level IV experiences. These experiences resemble what Dr. Abraham Maslow, the humanist psychologist, described as "peak experiences." Often the FEE makes surprising discoveries, arrives at amazing insights, attains new levels, and even acquires some clairvoyant sensitivity, at Level IV. Fully effective persons can expect some of these unusual and exciting insights frequently. The fully effective thought at Level IV is "Leave yourself open to surprising experiences."

In summary, FEEs use a combination of small talk, selective self-disclosure, productive listening, and openness to surprises as means of acquiring and sustaining their influencing skills.

FEEs know when to listen, but even more importantly, when not to listen. They know when to speak and when to keep quiet, when to put it in writing, and when to leave their pen in their pockets.

FEEs often ask themselves, "Should I be listening to this, or should I not be listening to this?" Whereas less effective persons often listen to everything, indiscriminately. Such persons often listen to the wrong thing or the wrong person at the wrong time or place. Listening to wrong persons, the wrong parts of what was said, or even worse, listening when nothing worthwhile is being said can be totally self-defeating. For example, Self-Defeating Pete Buyers swallowed wholesale the advice his colleagues at work gave him regarding his role in the company's new project. "I've got to stop pushing the company to expand. My friends told me so," Pete reminded himself. But Pete's "friends" were wrong. The project ultimately proved very successful, but poor Pete had backed out of it prematurely. If he had listened to his own gut reaction, rather than the opinion of his "friends" in this instance, he would have emerged a winner. With sufficient respect for his own feelings, his aggressive tactics would have had tremendous payoff, not only for him, but for his company as well.

FEE Larry Burns practices "productive listening." He sorts out those times when it makes sense to listen to others and when it doesn't. Larry trusts his own judgment considerably more than Pete Buyers does. Consequently, when Larry was advised by his boss to avoid conflicts with the competition, Larry resisted. "I believe my present directions still make sense," he explained, putting his job on the line. As a successful listener, Larry was attuned to his own inner drum beat. He knew intuitively when what he felt made sense, and therefore, came out a winner more often than not. "I tend always to give myself excellent advice. After all, I'm familiar with the case. I've been on this case for 42 years so far."

The Choice Is Always Yours: Use Execupower

Situation: Your daughter becomes emotional and distraught over a terrible argument she has just had with her college roommate. She phones you long distance and pleads with you to take her home right away. You listen.

Self-Defeating Thought	**Fully Effective Thought**
I listen only to content. My God she's really upset, I'll get her tickets to come home right away. This is terrible.	I listen to both content and feelings. I can appreciate her being upset. She is clearly very upset just now. I can listen primarily to her feelings and not attend to the content of what she is saying at this moment. However, if she still wants to come home a week from now, I might take her expressed desire to come home at face value.

FEEs listen according to the nature of the situations. They do not listen in the same way in all situations. When it pays to listen to content they do so. When it makes more sense to listen to feelings they do that, and when it's wise to tune out altogether, they do that too.

One beat and haggard psychiatrist ran into a very relaxed,

healthy looking friend whom he knew 25 years previously. They had both gone to the same medical school and later studied psychiatry together. "Well, hello Dr. Daniel Martin," the first psychiatrist said to his old friend. "You look absolutely wonderful. No wrinkles at all. You look as if life has been extremely easy. Look at me; I'm a haggard wreck. My psychiatric practice is killing me. All these years, listening every day to all my patients' complaints and aggravations. Absolutely killing. But you, Dan, you look wonderful. Hasn't being a psychiatrist gotten to you? Hasn't listening to all your patients' problems drained you? What's your secret?"

The other psychiatrist, Dr. Martin, replied with an easy smile, "Who listens?" Of course, this is an exaggeration, but the point is clear. If paying attention is of no consequence, FEEs will often take it upon themselves to tune out and thus preserve their inner selves.

FEE Neil Evans explained that sometimes intensive listening can harm others. "Sincere listening can sometimes cause a great deal of harm. Supposing that someone is very boring and you listen to that person attentively; are you being honest? No. The very act of your attentive listening only serves to reinforce his boring behavior. Sometimes it's more honest to yawn, right in front of such an individual. That way, at least, you give him the benefit of honest feedback."

The Choice Is Always Yours: Use Execupower

Situation: One of your staff members is reaching out to you for emotional help.

Self-Defeating Thought
I listen to everyone and everything with a critical ear.

Fully Effective Thought
I listen differently to different persons in various situations. I sometimes listen to feelings, other times to content, and other times just for pleasure. This time, it's for feelings.

Listening for content requires analytical skill. The FEE's sharp critical thinking ability allows him to avoid being taken in by form over substance. FEEs know that words often obfuscate rather than clarify, that many things are rarely just as they appear to be on the surface.

Listening for feelings requires a mindset of empathy, not critical analysis. FEE John Miller: "Many business people have never been listened to at the deepest level. Some people have never been heard on their own terms in their entire life." Even in marriage, there are cases of couples, who have been married for 15, 20, even 30 years, who have yet to really hear each other at a feelings level. Listening to feelings is probably more difficult to do than listening to content. FEEs focus on listening to feelings because that kind of listening helps them become closer to others, to friends, employees, family, and lovers.

In order to go about listening to feelings one must put into practice genuine caring plus offer accurate empathy for the person who is sharing. Martin Buber, a renowned philosopher, describes an "I-Thou" attitude that reflects genuine caring. With an "I-Thou" attitude as opposed to an "I-It" attitude, one totally appreciates a human being he is listening to. An "I-Thou" encounter is a very special event, where from the perspective of eternity, two human beings encounter each other at a given moment in time. "I-Thou" requires two individuals in their brief journey through time to genuinely care and appreciate each other as someone very special. "I-Thou" encounters can be awesome when one is reminded that for a given instant two persons journeying through time at a given moment become close, sharing common communication together. An "I-Thou" encounter rises above ethnic differences, social position, and all of the other relatively less important aspects that go with being simply a human being.

In order to have an "I-Thou" encounter, you must, for the moment, completely appreciate the individuality of the person you are listening to. None of the usual posturing that goes on so often in business is necessary or productive during "I-Thou" encounters.

The second ingredient that makes for deep listening is accurate empathy, with emphasis on the adjective *accurate*.

For example, assume that an employee attempts to share with you his upset regarding the fact that one of his children is very sick. If you have not suffered sufficiently in your own life, it can be extremely difficult for you to accurately empathize with that individual. All FEEs have permitted themselves to experience some suffering, garnering plenty of experience with the pain and anguish that is part of life. Experiences with difficult emotions permit them to identify with, and accurately connect with, the feelings of other persons who are sharing their difficulties.

While it is obviously quite unnecessary to undergo brain surgery just because the person whom you want to help is going through such an operation, it is still possible to extrapolate from your own life experiences aspects of suffering that are very similar to the feelings the person you are listening to is experiencing!

But FEEs never mistakenly use sympathy to replace empathy when they deeply listen. Sympathy means feeling *for,* while empathy means feeling *with.* While sympathy might be better than not caring at all about another person, accurate empathy, not sympathy, is what is really needed. The sympathetic executive says, "John, I feel sorry for you, what a shame." The empathetic FEE says, "John, I feel with you. I'm not you, but at the very least I can come close to experiencing just what you are feeling right now." John, upon receiving "I-Thou" respect plus accurate empathy from the FEE will tend to feel appreciated, cared for, and helped, whereas with only sympathy, a somewhat holier-than-thou attitude is conveyed. "Poor you" is not nearly as effective a type of listening as an "I-Thou," accurate empathy type of listening.

The Choice Is Always Yours: Use Execupower

Situation: One of your staff complains privately to you about the outrageous behavior of your boss, "old baggy pants."

Self-Defeating Thought	Fully Effective Thought
I love hearing this. Tell me more about old baggy pants. (or) Stop, please. You can't speak disloyally about the boss this way.	This person is simply sharing feelings with me. I'll listen to his feelings and bear in mind that the issues is feelings, rather than substance. It's sometimes healthy to let a person bitch, if he does so with discretion.

FEEs sometimes deliberately try to create tension in business or political encounters. They may stand up and leave when another person is speaking excessively. On other occasions, FEEs sometimes deliberately misunderstand the content or the feelings of what a speaker shares, if it makes sense to do so. FEEs may even slightly distort what a speaker has said, deliberately putting words in the speaker's mouth. These tactics, of course, are only used to disconcert. FEEs use defensive ploys of this type only on those rare occasions when a good offense serves as the best defense.

Although FEEs attend and usually lead numerous meetings, they never suffer at boring meetings. At such meetings, FEEs listen only to what is appropriate. FEEs are masters of tuning in and tuning out as needed. If a child is disruptive, or a spouse nags, he simply tunes out. If there is serious business at a meeting, he tunes in. If his secretary complains without justification, he tunes out again. However, no one would ever know any of this if they depended on the FEE's facial expressions or body language. He really knows how to hide his inner feelings, whenever it makes sense to do so. FEE Ron Davies: "In business, it's not always wise to wear your feelings on your sleeve."

Once I had a professor who was not entirely joking when he said, "If you want to get your Ph.D., the trick is to take a seat in the front row, look the professor in the eye periodically, nod affirmatively, and say 'how true, how true.' "

FEEs conserve their limited energies by listening only when it really makes sense to listen. While productive listening was considered much more important than speaking, according to

FEEs, they had similar ideas about speaking too. FEEs always weigh their words in business.

Kahlil Gibran, author of *The Prophet,* wrote: "We speak when we are no longer at peace with our thoughts." Since FEEs are not compulsive about needing to speak, and since their thoughts provide them with sufficient inner calm, they are skilled in knowing exactly when to and when not to talk. When a person speaks indiscriminately, after a time his words lose much of their impact. FEEs speak crisply and to the point, rather than saying too much for no particular reason. When FEEs do speak, they speak convincingly. FEE Jim Geary: "Sometimes when I hear myself talking, I'm very impressed. There have been times when I've been nervous; then heard my calm-sounding voice and the sound of it, my own voice, I actually calmed down."

FEEs write to influence too, but they avoid putting those things in writing that are better left unwritten. Although FEEs often keep private notes for themselves, they keep corporate memo writing to a bare minimum. Especially memos to peers. On those occasions when they address a memo to their own boss, it is exceptionally well prepared.

In summary, FEEs influence others, but they don't try to control them, preferring to develop intrinsic motivation in others, rather than extrinsic motivation. They productively influence by presenting a strong image and convincing ideas; they use their excellent communication skills to work through, with, and for others as they move toward corporate and personal success.

Drawing on the FEE's Influence Practice, what fully effective thoughts apply to the following situations?

- You have a compelling urge to speak out strongly at a company meeting regarding certain controversial issues.
- You are "required" to attend a party at the boss's home in honor of a colleague you've long disliked.
- Your spouse is furious because you didn't speak up in her behalf while with another couple. She says that once again you showed that you only care about yourself.

- You are nervous about giving a talk to the executive staff. Your entire future depends on how well you make this presentation.

Influence pays off, but influence without a game plan makes little sense. Hence the FEE's Strategist Practice is next.

9

THE STRATEGIST PRACTICE

Fully Effective Thought #5: "Be a Gamesman, Not a Street Fighter."

FEEs know how to play the interesting games of making money and getting ahead in business, as well as the infinitely more serious game of life. They play both games to win, but make a clear differentiation between the two, never taking business so seriously that they spoil their lives. One thing FEEs take very seriously is their hidden identity, with its built-in elements of inner calm, purpose, and adventure. "I'm determined to have calm, purpose, and adventure in my life, no matter what," FEEs say.

Their top priority goal, "to have a very satisfying personal and professional life" is never compromised. But making money, working, moving ahead in the organization, getting newer and better jobs, are arenas where they have excitement and fun. They never lose sight of their major objective, always making sure that they enjoy life as they move along achieving their material goals with relative ease. Since making money, getting promoted, etc. are not entirely under the FEEs' control, and therefore can't be guaranteed, they find it essential not to take them as seriously as their top goal, "life satisfaction." Paradoxically, the FEE, as a skilled tactician and strategist, tends to achieve his material objectives primarily by not trying too hard.

The Choice Is Always Yours: Use Execupower

Situation: You are offered a promotion to "staff," but "line," not staff, is the road to the top in your organization.

Self-Defeating Thought
I'll take it. A bird in hand is worth two in the bush.

Fully Effective Thought
I'll let it go, I know exactly what I'm after. If I don't get what I want, it won't be a disaster. But I'm shooting for the top within the next six years.

FEE Dick Barnes: "Please don't let anyone know. If the people back at my company ever found out how lightly I take my job, they'd feel very much let down. They enjoy thinking of me as a workaholic. You see, my game plan calls for me to act earnest, as if everything that happens within the company really matters. So sometimes when things go wrong, I feign worry and upset. They love it. Sometimes I act angry just to get my people up and moving. Acting angry can be productive, but really being angry usually makes very little sense. Down deep, I never forget that there are many, many more important things in this world than the production of high quality widgets and the making of profits. This world will be here long after the company, its products, and I have ceased to exist.

"I never stop reminding myself that I have deeper purposes and meaning in my life than mere business success. Since it's my life, and I only have one life to live, I intend to make it the most satisfying life possible. I'm out to win the world's record for inner satisfaction. What surprises me is that I haven't had to sacrifice job success at all, nor have I had to neglect the company's interests one iota to achieve my goal. I love being the boss, making plenty of money, and enjoying all the perks that go with being top dog. I love it. But success in business is not crucial in order for me to have my terrific life."

Many FEEs have clearly achieved their material success with relative ease in spite of the fact that material success was not their top objective. Why is it that most persons who want nothing more than more money, power, and prestige cannot seem to get it? Is it because they want it so badly that they cramp their own style? FEEs like to win. But they always know exactly what it is that they are after.

FEE Ted Barton: "Power to me means getting what I want, or at least getting what I want done by somebody else. That's all that power is. Consequently, when I get what I want, I feel powerful. However, if I don't seem to be making progress toward getting what I want, then I feel powerless. What can be even worse than getting nothing is getting something I never really ever wanted in the first place. That's why I always am clear to myself as to what I'm really after. I'm very likely to get it."

FEEs always have a game plan in mind. It sometimes appears at first glance that they have lost, only to find out later that they have won. The prize that is on display is not always the one that they are really after. FEEs have a way of feeling victorious, no matter what.

Even the roles played in the FEE's family life are often considered part of a pleasurable game. They take their roles as husband, wife, father, brother, etc., as just that, roles to be played, not roles to suffer with. They make a fine distinction between the jobs that they do and the roles that they play. For example, they're serious about "fathering" as a job that needs doing to help their child.

But "father" is never who they really are at the deepest level. Hence, they usually play the role of father with ease.

The Choice Is Always Yours: Use Execupower

Situation: An opportunity to head an important committee comes your way, but in your estimation, acceptance of this responsibility will sidetrack you from attaining more important personal goals.

Self-Defeating Thought	**Fully Effective Thought**
I'll do it. I can do everything. If I do something well, by all means I should do it.	I'll turn it down. I'm honored that I've been asked and I believe that I could do a good job. But still, I can't do everything that comes my way. I edit my life with emphasis on quality over quantity.

FEEs see the bigger picture and therefore compete with others to win/win, rather than to win/lose. Win/win often involves negotiation, forming coalitions of interest groups that have mutual ties rather than fighting with "the enemy" in order to win. Whenever necessary, they pause, then choose fully effective, strategic thoughts, thoughts that are in tune with their "big picture" game plan. How many have won the battle only to find out later that they've lost the war?

The Choice Is Always Yours: Use Execupower

Situation: Your family misses you. You're spending too much time away from home.

Self-Defeating Thought	**Fully Effective Thought**
I owe my 'all' to the company yet I want to get ahead for my	I only pass this way once, and I've got to edit my life. I

(*Self-Defeating Thought*)	(*Fully Effective Thought*)
family's sake.	can't be all things to all people. And I can only be in one place at a time. I owe my family a fair shake. My family and I will have a long talk about our mutual goals and how we can reach them together.

Maultsby, in *The Gamesman,* described executives who play to win, but who always play with a poker face. FEEs have a bit of the poker player in them too. They maintain a poker face as they do their very best with the cards they have been dealt. They know when to go for broke, or call for a new deal, and they can always handle their losses. While they truly enjoy winning, they play essentially for fun. Most importantly, they always play with a full deck, bearing in mind the important goals that they are really after.

FEE Ted Rogers: "I need to work with and through people in my business. Therefore, I always try to find people who have the special talent to do the particular job that I need to get done. Since all persons are motivated primarily by their own self-interests, I make it my business to find out what their interests are. Then I set it up so that I'm viewed as the one who can help them get what they want. If they see me as that somebody who controls their getting what they want, I usually have them under my influence. That's how I get power. In this business [TV production] most of the people in it are in it for fame and fortune. And I'm powerful only because these people see me as the gatekeeper who presides over whether they get their share of fame and fortune or not. I enjoy this business for what it is, just a game. If I ever took it seriously, I couldn't last in it."

The Choice Is Always Yours: Use Execupower

Situation: You do not have enough authority to carry out your extensive job responsibilities.

Self-Defeating Thought
My power comes essentially from the authority attributed to my position in the organizational structure. I've been extremely shortchanged. I'm very handicapped.

Fully Effective Thought
Most of my power is personal power. My power over others comes essentially from my awareness of other people's self-interests. Therefore, I have to care about what other people want. Then I serve their interests to the extent that I can. I manage this job effectively, while at the same time do whatever I have to do to get more official authority from the company to carry out my responsibilities even more effectively. I'm never a victim.

It's the people who don't know what they really want who are the most difficult persons for FEEs to handle. FEE Jack Miller: "Once I know what somebody is after, I can readily manage him. But if he's confused, if he doesn't know his own mind, then I have to create goals for him. Confused persons are the most difficult for me. It's hard to know what they are after, so they're difficult to manage." FEEs use their keen awareness of people's self-interests to help them create successful work teams.

FEE Vera Jennings: "Here at the hospital there are five conflicting groups, each with its own goals. I've figured out how to organize them into coalitions. What I did was to find unconflicting self-interests that each of them had and then I combined each group with a compatible group so that they could both work toward a common objective. As an administrator, my biggest job is negotiating coalitions so that everyone around here can win. Especially the patients. After all, it's because of the patients that we're here."

FEEs use their Strategist Practice to get what they want from their bosses, their subordinates, their peers, their spouse, and even from their children.

FEE Don Heath: "My boss is motivated out of his own self-interests, just like me, just like anybody else. So I sat down one day and I said to myself: 'Don, what does that crazy boss of yours really want?' Then I answered, 'He wants the very same things that you want from your subordinates. He wants total loyalty from you. He wants somebody who he can unconditionally trust. He also wants plenty of recognition from his boss.' Every boss has a boss, even mine. Sure I'm the president of this damn company, but even I have five or six bosses. I report to the C.E.O. and even he reports to the Chairman of the Board. Accountability never stops. My boss only wants to make a good impression on his boss. So since I want to get what I want out of my boss, I just make damned sure that he gets plenty of credit for whatever I do that is good. And I always make it clear to him that I am totally loyal to his interests. He respects me for that. I've learned a few things over the years, much of it the hard way. I've not become president here out of nowhere."

The Choice Is Always Yours: Use Execupower

Situation: That promotion you were hoping for has fallen through.

Self-Defeating Thought	**Fully Effective Thought**
This company is a people-grinder. I hate it here.	This company is like most organizations. I'll work hard for it while I'm here, but as always, my eyes are open for better opportunities. America's a free market. I always keep my resume updated and ready for action. It's plan B time.

FEE Loretta Reese explains how she gets what she wants from her colleagues and subordinates, "I want loyalty and a good day's work out of my staff. Therefore, it's necessary for me to identify with what they want from me, and get it for them. My workers, more than anything else, want to be treated fairly, with respect and appreciation. Fairness is their biggest issue. As the boss, I'm a parental figure and therefore I always treat 'my people' fairly, equally. They appreciate that and do a great job for me. But if I'm ever unfair, or even perceived as being unfair, watch out!"

FEE Herb Ditton: "I have a long-standing policy to reprimand in private and always commend in public. All people need and want dignity. And I give it to them, and in turn, get done what I want to get done!" If you find out what your colleagues really want, and get it for them, you'll probably have excellent peer relationships at work. Colleagues might undercut you if they find you too threatening. What colleagues often want from you is a simple sense that you won't undermine them, threaten their turf, or 'mess' with company job norms. If you're on a fast track, you might be resented for spoiling the norms. The best advice, here, is to go easy! Keep a relatively low profile with colleagues and be sure never to brag. All people are interested in their own progress. To the extent that you can be helpful and share good ideas, you'll be appreciated.

Getting what you want from a spouse, lover, or friends is, once again, a matter of finding out what they want and then putting yourself in the position to get it for them. Most intimate friends want someone who really cares for them, listens to them, and appreciates them on their own terms. They thrive on such a friend's caring relationship. Since FEEs know to listen deeply to feelings when appropriate, they easily build excellent, warm, close relationships with selected individuals, especially family and one or two close friends.

Below are some situations that can be dealt with most effectively through application of the Strategist Practice. What tactics would you recommend for each of the following?

- While traveling together to a meeting, your boss asks you to tell him confidentially what you really think of him, that he won't hold anything against you. All he wants is your honest opinion. You think he is quite overbearing at meetings. Should you tell him?

- Your spouse is unreasonably jealous of you and expressing suspicions that you've had too many nights "working late."
- You hope to get promoted but you have insufficient visibility in your present role. What can you do to get a higher profile?

Strategically, looking at the total picture, it's now time to sharpen your decision making skills. Next and last, the FEE's Decisiveness Practice.

10

THE DECISIVENESS PRACTICE

Fully Effective Thought #6:
"Plan Carefully, Then Decide Wisely and with Dispatch."

FEEs make wise decisions rapidly. They advance in their personal life and in business, not because the world is especially kind to them, but because they make many more wise decisions then poor ones.

Their decisions prove successful because they do all their homework well in advance, not because they are just lucky. FEE Phillip Roberts: "The better I plan, the luckier I get."

FEEs determine exactly what it is they are after; then they go for it. Their personal and professional goals always go hand in hand. They never forget, even for a moment, that their top priority objective is to have "one of the most satisfying lives ever had by anybody." None of their decisions are permitted to conflict with this heartfelt primary life objective. Whenever an opportunity to advance toward one of their objectives presents itself, FEEs are instantly ready to act, intuitively and wisely.

For example, if an FEE were to be interested in real estate, he might make it his business to know a genuine real estate bargain when one presented itself. He'd be on the alert, perhaps, for houses with tarnished exteriors. Houses that with some fresh paint and new siding could command a good price in the real estate market. Then when this FEE happened to spot such a bargain, he would be ready to decide wisely and to act with dispatch, while other persons who don't know what they are after drive right by such potential bargains simply because they aren't on the alert.

If FEEs genuinely want to make plenty of money, they systematically study finance. Since FEEs always concentrate on enjoying their lives, they go about that just as systematically. Their antennae are always attuned to opportunities that are in keeping with their personal and professional objectives.

The human brain is composed of two hemispheres, right and left. The left hemisphere produces all of our logical thinking. The right hemisphere is the origin of our creative thinking. FEEs use both sides. They plan carefully with their left brain and decide spontaneously, creatively, with their right.

FEE Vera Jennings: "I was thirty-one years old, and I figured it was time to get a good man for myself. I decided I wanted someone who was a compassionate lover. In order to find someone who fit these criteria of mine, I positioned myself so that I would physically be in the vicinity of such a person and that I'd be interesting and attractive to him. I figured that if I situated myself in the vicinity of the type of man I wanted, I'd have a much better than average chance to snare one than if I just trusted solely to chance. I wanted to set the odds distinctly in my favor. So I took a job as an administrator of a busy law office in a wealthy suburban community—a community where there were plenty of opportunities to meet the type of man I intended to meet. Eventually, after a while, I met Frank Lauton. This was four years ago. Last year Frank and I decided to get married and

I think it's been one of the best 'spontaneous' decisions I ever made. Wasn't I lucky?" she asked with a wry wink.

All FEEs make their own breaks, whether it's in finding jobs, in planning their careers, or in landing a spouse. They plan their financial objectives well in advance and the kind of working environments they want to spend time in. They even seek out ahead of time the best geographic locations for finding work of their choice. FEE Dick Barnes: "I don't wait for the mountain to come to Mohammed. I go out to the world, and get from the world pretty much what I want. Elias Howe invented the sewing machine. But he died a poor man, because he mistakenly thought the world would beat a path to his door. Nothing really happens by osmosis."

When an FEE makes a decision, it is a whole body, right-brain process. FEE Loretta Reese: "Did you ever go to a store and try on a coat? It looks good at first, but something inside you tells you that this coat, somehow, just isn't right for you. A little bell goes off inside me that says, 'Bong. This coat just isn't right for you.' Or, 'Yes, it's just right for you.' That little bell tells me whether I should buy the coat or put it back on the rack. If I listen to that bell very carefully, I never make a mistaken decision. But if I don't pause for a moment and listen for it—that's when I usually go wrong. It's as if my whole body is speaking to me. All I have to do is listen."

FEEs listen to their own subconscious in order to make their most important decisions. They plan carefully, then ask their wise subconscious for the decision: "Should we expand to a broader market?" "Should we relocate the plant?" "Should I hire that new worker?" "Should I marry that woman?" They ask their right brain for answers and they listen to the advice they get from inside. If FEEs diet, they plan ahead before they decide what to eat. Since most decisions must be made before all the facts are in, the FEE's systematic advance planning prepares him to decide intuitively, with only those facts that were available at decision-making time.

Speed in decision-making, especially in business, is always an advantage. Certain opportunities present themselves only once, then totally disappear. If you're not preprogrammed to take advantage of these special opportunities and take calculated risks, you will obviously miss out.

The Choice Is Always Yours: Use Execupower

Situation: You have a chance to make some big money on a wild speculation.

Self-Defeating Thought	**Fully Effective Thought**
I'll play it safe.	I'll look at it and let my intuition be my guide. I already know what my goals are and my subconscious can tell me whether to risk it or not.

The following are some decisions you might consider if you have done your pre-decision homework:

(1) Invest heavily into the stock market right now.
(2) Change your job.
(3) Ask for a big raise or a promotion.
(4) Buy a new home, or move.
(5) Go into business for yourself right away.
(6) Invest in a real estate speculation.
(7) Adopt a needy child.
(8) Take that big vacation trip you so well deserve.
(9) Take up that hobby that you've been putting off—artwork, painting, sculpting, playing a musical instrument, learning a foreign language, skydiving, or joining a little theater group.

All of these potential decisions require advance planning on your part. In order to make wise decisions, the following seven-step procedure can be extremely useful. After using it a few times, each step will become habitual. FEEs intuitively use these steps to make their decisions.

(1) Remind yourself of your success goals (as established earlier) and bear these goals in mind as you go through the remaining steps. Be certain not to forget your top priority objective, "having a very satisfying life."

(2) Briefly state the issue that requires your decision.

(3) List those factors that precipitated the need for a decision now.

(4) Brainstorm as many options as you can before you attempt to make your final decision.

(5) Select the one option that seems best from your list of available options.

(6) Consider the probable outcome of this option.

(7) If it sits well with you, try it. Act on it. If it doesn't sit well with you, try selecting another option for consideration.

The following Wise Decisions Checklist should help you make wise decisions. Select a genuine issue that currently requires a decision and complete the chart.

Wise Decisions Checklist

_____1. Remind yourself of your major personal and professional goals. (See "Charting Your Success Goals" in Chapter 3.) Remember, your top priority goal should be to have "one of the most satisfying lives possible, and not at the expense of any other person." Continue to bear your success goals in mind as you complete the remaining steps. Your goals are:

_____

_____

_____

_____2. Briefly state the one issue that presently requires your decision.

_____

_____

_____

_____3. Why is a decision about this issue useful now?

_____

_____

_____4. What options are available to you? List all of the options you can think of, using your own shorthand. Possible decision options:

_____

_____

_____5. The one decision that seems among the most attractive is as follows (describe succinctly, but clearly):

_____

_____

_____6. Predict the probable outcome after having taken this decision option:

_____

_____

_____7. Ask yourself, "Am I comfortable with this idea?" If it sits well with your intuition, act on it emphatically.

_____

_____

_____

Risking a decision requires that you sense whether or not you are deciding in complete harmony with the success goals that you've established for yourself. Will your deciding bring you closer to achieving your objectives? If "yes," take action. Otherwise stop and reconsider your other options. One option may be "no decision right now." Of course, not deciding is a decision too.

Once you've decided to act, it's time to consider the very worst that can happen. Can you afford to fail or will failure be totally disastrous? FEEs believe in advance that they will be able to deal effectively with whatever the outcome might be. "I can always choose thoughts that will permit me to survive in reasonable mental health," they say. While they might need to draw on the Execupower Principle and also use their inner identity to feel okay, resort to the ABCs of choosing, or remind themselves of the Reality Practice, the Eustress Practice, or any other tactic now available to them through Execupower—they will inevitably end up saying to themselves, "I don't need to preoccupy myself with failure since I can always handle it. Therefore, I can move forward now."

After figuring out how you can readily handle failure, it's time to go forward, time to visualize success. See success, smell it, taste it. Then act emphatically. Risk it. Give it your best shot. Once you put this seven-step system into operation regularly, rapid wise decision making will become a habit. But at first, proceed deliberately until these seven steps become second nature to you.

If an FEE contemplates changing jobs, he asks himself how this decision is likely to affect the balance of his life purpose and adventure. "Would taking this new job be likely to improve my level of inner calm?" "Would the change add to the quality of adventure in my life?" "To what extent would this job change move me toward the major purposes of my life as I presently see them?" If, in the mind of the FEE, there is sufficient support to predict that a job change will increase his inner satisfaction over the long run, he would seriously consider chancing the new job. But if the effects seem likely to spoil his inner balance, he'll let the opportunity pass.

If a given risk seems to be too dangerous, so dangerous that it probably will effectively reduce his inner calm for a long time, or if it isn't sufficiently exciting, adding to his adventure, the FEE will table his final decision. He resists interfering too much with the quality of his inner life over any extended period of time, and always reminds himself that a balance of inner calm, purpose, and adventure are essential if he is to enjoy his life.

The FEE continuously asks himself, "What will this decision do to the quality of my inner life if I succeed or if I fail?" They will never compromise the quality of their inner life no matter how much material gain, riches, or fame is dangled in front of them.

The Choice Is Always Yours: Use Execupower

Situation: An important report is due next week but you can't stop procrastinating.

Self-Defeating Thought	Fully Effective Thought
Think positive. It'll get done somehow.	Think negative. I'd better get my tail in gear or I won't have that report ready on time.

FEEs always calculate whether a particular risk is worth taking or not. To pass another car on a wet, dangerous, narrow highway makes little sense. Sometimes, obviously, you just can't afford the loss. However, there are certain risks that appear to be foolish at first glance, but later turn out to be worthwhile.

FEE Don Heath: "After I graduated from college, I decided to join the U.S. Air Force. I wanted to be a pilot ever since I was a kid, and was thrilled to be accepted into the academy. But I flunked out after the first month. What a shock. What a disappointment! At the time, it was absolutely traumatic. Imagine. All my childhood dreams, shattered. However, after awhile, I picked up the pieces and made a new start for myself; and I never really let go of my dream. I felt that I was grounded, but only temporarily. That early disappointment caused me to think a lot more than I ever did before in my entire life. That failure made me a whole lot wiser about life. I learned from pain and suffering. It took me a lot longer, but now I've got my pilot's license, yet I've never forgotten what I learned from my failure back then. Learning to deal with failure, by actually failing myself, made me a much more compassionate person. My decision to take training looked as if it was all wrong. After all, I flunked out. But now, looking back, that decision has proven to be one of the wisest decisions I ever made in my entire life. There's nothing wrong with making a bad decision, if we can learn from it."

The Choice Is Always Yours: Use Execupower

Situation: You finally hit paydirt from that risky venture you initiated some time ago.

Self-Defeating Thought	Fully Effective Thought
I'm so lucky. I wouldn't have gotten it without the encouragement of others.	I made it happen. Others helped and I appreciate that. But it never would have happened if I alone didn't initiate the venture.

Once you figure out exactly how to handle a loss, both emotionally and materially, you are ready to take the risk. FEE Ted Rogers: "All I really own is my body and my mind, and the thoughts I choose; the rest is really rented." FEEs view material possessions as transitory things they use for a time and then let go of. They consistently remind themselves of the old cliche, "You can't take it with you." In that way, they keep material things from owning them, from running their lives. They believe they really own something only when they've overcome the fear of ever losing it.

The Choice Is Always Yours: Use Execupower

Situation: An opportunity for quick advancement suddenly confronts you. You must act quickly if you are to take advantage of it.

Self-Defeating Thought	Fully Effective Thought
I must make a rapid decision. But I'm not ready. Let it pass.	This ties in precisely with my plans. My intuition tells me to go for it—now!

Since FEEs are productive, they tend to attract productive people to work with them. Persons who know exactly what they want out of their life tend to be attractive. Those FEEs that were married tended to have good marriages. They apparently made wise mating decisions. Few people seem to make personal life decisions that prove more satisfying than those made by FEEs.

FEEs are successful in their mating decisions because they plan ahead, using left-brain logic. They planned ahead as to what kind of person they would enjoy living with and would like to marry, and then they used their right brain to instinctively make the decision to marry.

The Choice Is Always Yours: Use Execupower

Situation: The constant striving to make more money is clearly getting the best of you. You never seem to be making enough. You feel as if you are on a treadmill.

Self-Defeating Thought	**Fully Effective Thought**
I can truly own many things.	All I truly own is my mind, my body, and my thoughts. Every material possession I have is really just rented. Ownership is merely an illusion, since I can never take it with me. I own the sky, my senses, my feelings, my thoughts. I need a modicum of food, shelter, and clothing for my family and me. But *enough* is simply an attitude that I can choose.

FEEs generally take more risks than the average person because of their "I can handle the loss" attitude. Once an FEE decides to go for it, he puts failure completely out of his mind. FEEs approach strangers, authority figures, prospective clients, and business opportunities with relative ease simply because they're not at all afraid of rejection or failure.

FEE Phil Roberts: "In approaching an attractive woman across the room, I wonder for a moment, should I really be doing this? It could be embarrassing if I'm rejected. But then I ask myself, 'What could be the worst thing that could happen to me?' She could say, 'Please leave, I don't want to talk to you' or 'Kindly leave me alone.' If that happens, why, I'm in exactly the same position I was in in the first place. I'll certainly not fall to the ground in a dead faint. I figure that I can handle the rejection if it comes. Then I say to myself, 'Okay, Phil, go for it. Meet and greet that beautiful woman.'"

People who are not afraid of risk usually meet with eventual success. Those who never take chances might never get hurt, but they will also achieve relatively little.

You're playing golf. The green is 140 yards away over a large pond. What's the worst that can happen? What will happen to you if your ball lands in the pond? Can you handle the embarrassment, the cost of the ball, the penalties? If so, why not go for it?

Envision yourself as Jack Nicklaus or Nancy Lopez taking that perfect swing, landing the ball gently onto the green. Actually see yourself performing in optimal fashion. Effective thoughts will bring your whole body into action.

Here's an important activity that you should complete in one day. Doing this will virtually guarantee that you'll improve your decision-making skills. Go out and take a big, productive risk within the next 24 hours. Don't be afraid to fail. You'll learn a tremendous amount either way.

How would you apply effective thinking to following decisions?

- Should you ask your boss for a raise (or a promotion, a better office, etc.)?
- Should you treat yourself to an expensive item that you've long wanted and well deserve?
- Should you call the travel agent and book that well-earned vacation?
- Should you risk investing right now?

• When are you going to begin that project you've long had in mind (writing, building, repairing, etc.)?

Remember, even if you find everything you've learned about Execupower very interesting, you will still only fully **understand** Execupower when you put it into action.

And now—graduation.

11

GRADUATION:
Reaping All the Fantastic
Benefits of Execupower

The Execupower System in review is pictured below:

THE EXECUPOWER PRINCIPLE

With Execupower you have at your disposal all that is necessary for you to achieve and sustain your own high level of three-dimensional success, the job you want, the capacity to really enjoy that job, and the means for an extremely satisfying personal life as well.

Any time you run into difficulty, put Execupower into action. Remind yourself to *pause,* then choose fully effective thoughts, thoughts derived from the six practices of FEEs.

Here's how a hypothetical person, "Tom," used the Execupower Worksheet to deal with the upset that occurred when his house was robbed and some of his most valuable possessions were taken.

Tom's Execupower Worksheet

(1) Briefly describe the disturbing condition that currently concerns you.

My house was robbed last night. Many of my most valuable possessions were taken: my photo album, TV, jewelry etc.

(2) What practical external steps can you take to ameliorate or remedy the situation?

- called the police already   - thinking of getting a watch dog - we've searched for clues - am installing a burglar alarm - leaving lights and radio on from now on.

(3) What Fully Effective Thoughts can best serve you in view of the prevailing situation?

I didn't really own anything but my mind and body. All possessions are really just rented. Can't take them with me. I'm on vacation from eternity. Life is finite. Live a F-UL life, not a FOOL's life. Seek eustress not distress. etc. etc.

(4) What Self-Defeating Thoughts are you having that need to be quelled?

My possessions are gone and are irreplaceable. I especially treasured my photos. I've been treated so unfairly and deserve much better. I'm decent. Why isn't everyone else?

All of the effective thoughts that Tom chose were derived from the six practices of FEEs—the Reality, Hidden Identity, Eustress, Influence, Strategist, and Decisiveness Practices. And now this system is yours to use as you see fit.

About three weeks after you've been putting Execupower to work for you, take the Fully Effective Self-Test (Chapter 2) once again. Your scores will be much improved by then, and if there are still a few areas of weakness left, all you need do is simply return to the parts of this book that have a particular application in the area of effectiveness that you are upgrading. Using Execupower consistently can help bring you fantastic benefits—perhaps a bigger and better job, genuine enjoyment of that job, and an excellent personal life as well.

Although the FEEs in this book must remain anonymous for obvious reasons, there is one "FEE-like" person whose actual identity I can reveal to you. That person is my father, Benjamin Kushel. Three years ago, he retired as president of a prospering savings and loan company in my hometown. Fifteen years previous to his work in banking, he and my mother ran a very busy delicatessen for more than 30 years.

I realize that I cannot be completely objective about my own father, but I do know him extremely well; I've known him all my life.

Although my father never formally studied psychology, as I have, and will probably never write a book such as this, he, in my view, puts the Execupower Principle into action every day. He always makes certain that he has a very satisfying day, each and every day of his life, and continues to do so as long as he lives. It's his way.

When my father was 58, after undergoing stomach surgery, the surgeon called me aside and whispered, "Get his affairs in order. Don't let him get involved in anything. He's definitely got no more than six months left to live. He's got cancer of the pancreas."

Needless to say, that was extremely disheartening news, but my father didn't know about the doctor's diagnosis. He returned home from the hospital, sold the delicatessen, and we waited for him to die. Instead, he proceeded to get healthier and healthier; in fact, he became his robust self once again.

To make a long story short, he's now 87 years old, and the internist who diagnosed his case is long gone. My father, in what has always been his "FEE-like" custom, continues enjoying his satisfying personal and professional life.

During the 29 years that have passed since he was first diagnosed as having cancer (later considered cured by a miraculous spontaneous remission), my father worked his way up in the savings and loan business to eventually become president at age 72. "Don't peak too soon," he advises. "Peaking late in life gives you something to look forward to." The company's assets have more than quadrupled during his years as president, until just a few years ago. My mother died not too long ago and my father mourned appropriately and intensely, but only six months. Then he asked Blanche, a recent widow, to marry him. They spent a wonderful honeymoon in Hawaii.

Only one year after he remarried, my father had a stroke and of necessity resigned from the presidency of the savings and loan. He's formally retired now, but has once again made an excellent recovery from illness, thanks largely to his "FEE-like" attitude and Blanche's warm care.

While recovering from his stroke, he came with me to the WNYC radio studio in Manhattan, where I was conducting a call-in radio talk show. A woman from the Bronx had called in, complaining bitterly of her loneliness. "My children never call," she said. "No one seems to call. I'm so much alone."

My father ambled up to the studio microphone and without his only son's permission, took the mike in hand and said firmly, *"Lady, join clubs."* With that said, he ambled promptly back to his seat.

That is Execupower in a nutshell. Take the givens, pause, choose effective thoughts, and work it "positive" from there.

Time Now for an Execupower Review

(1) What are your major success goals? Remind yourself of your primary objective. (Chapter 3)

1. _____
2. _____
3. _____

(2) State the Execupower Principle

_____

(3) Remind yourself of the six basic effective thoughts that accompany each of the FEEs' practices.
   • The Reality Practice (Chapter 5)
       "Be realistic, not merely reasonable."
   • The Hidden Identity Practice (Chapter 6)
       "Use your hidden identity, not your job title or family role."
   • The Eustress Practice (Chapter 7)
       "Seek eustress, not distress."
   • The Influence Practice (Chapter 8)
       "Influence others, don't try to control them."
   • The Strategist Practice (Chapter 9)
       "Be a gamesman, not a street fighter."
   • The Decisiveness Practice (Chapter 10)
       "Plan carefully, then decide wisely."

(4) Complete the following:
   • Three things that I can realistically expect are:
       1. _____
       2. _____
       3. _____
   • My hidden identity is: _____
   • Calm, purpose, and adventure are structured into my hidden identity as follows:

       _____
       _____
       _____

   • Three areas in which I will seek eustress are:
       1. _____
       2. _____
       3. _____
   • I will use influence, not control, to achieve the following three objectives:
       1. _____
       2. _____

3. _____

- I will use strategies to achieve the following three objectives:
  1. _____
  2. _____
  3. _____

(5) State the ABCs of Choosing:
   A. _____
   B. _____
   C. _____

(6) Explain the value of living a F-U-L life, rather than a FOOL's life.
   F- _____
   U- _____
   L- _____

(7) What is "mourning in advance"? When is this method most useful?

_____

_____

(8) How is Calming Self-Talk best employed?

_____

_____

The Execupower Worksheet

(1) Briefly describe the disturbing condition that currently concerns you.

_____

_____

_____

(2) What practical external steps can you take to ameliorate or remedy the situation?

_____

_____

_____

(3) What Fully Effective Thoughts can best serve you in view of the prevailing situation?

_____

_____

_____

(4) What Self-Defeating Thoughts are you having that need to be
quelled?

_____

_____

_____

Remember to consistently use the Execupower Worksheet and
all the other aids that Execupower offers until operating as an
FEE becomes a matter of habit.

Realistically, Execupower sets you up to achieve 100% success
both personally and professionally. Remember, no matter what
life dishes up, you are always Chief Executive in charge of
yourself and the thoughts that you choose. Here's to your Total
Success! Be sure to enjoy your relatively short vacation from
eternity.

INDEX